GARTH BROOKS
THE ULTIMATE HITS

Alfred Music Publishing Co., Inc.
16320 Roscoe Blvd., Suite 100
P.O. Box 10003
Van Nuys, CA 91410-0003
alfred.com

ISBN-10: 1-7390-4949-6
ISBN-13: 978-0-7390-4949-5

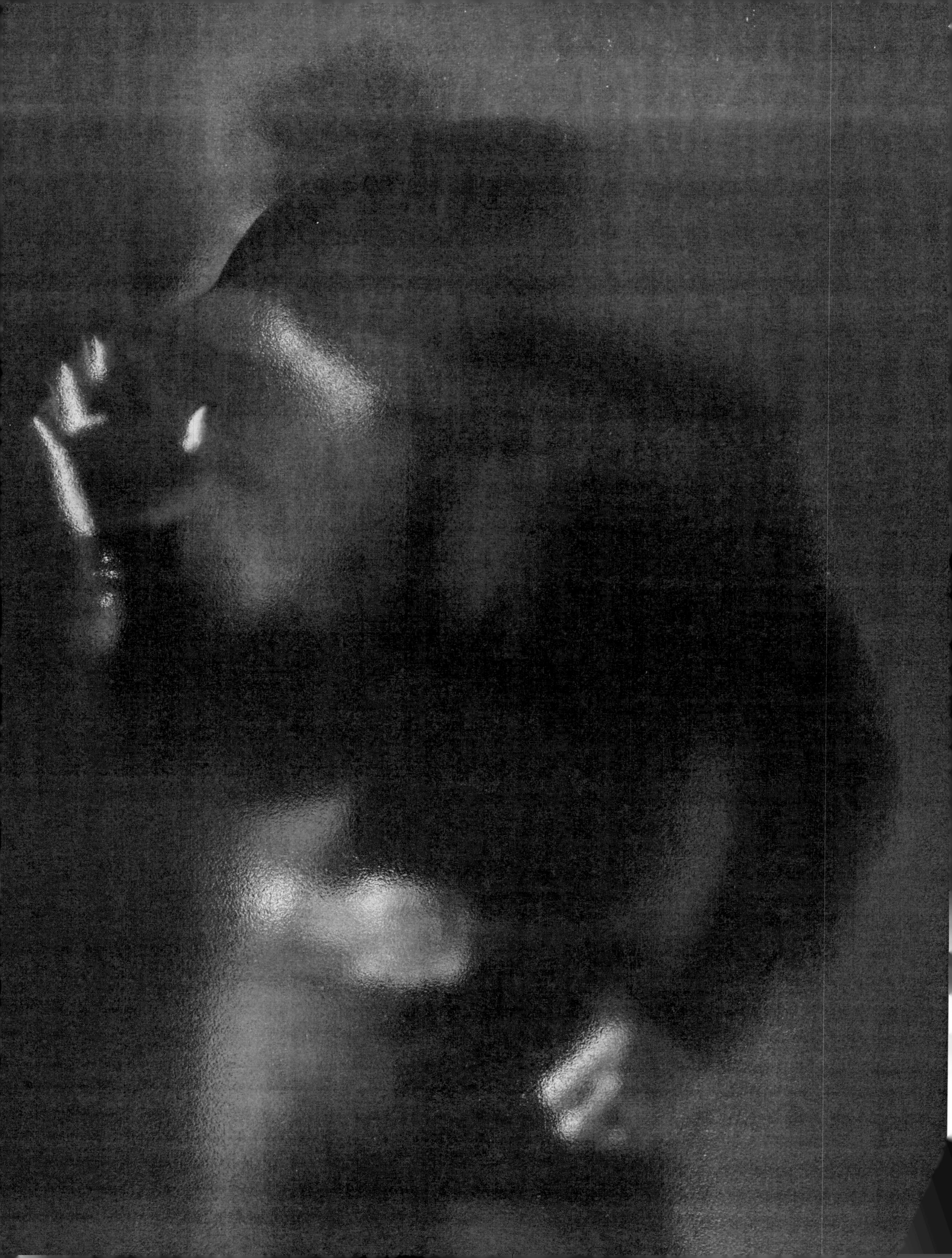

CONTENTS

AIN'T GOING DOWN ('TIL THE SUN COMES UP)

Words and Music by
KENT BLAZY, KIM WILLIAMS
and GARTH BROOKS

C5
Lo - cal coun - try sta - tion just a - blar - in' on the ra - di - o,
G5
pick him up at sev - en and they're head - in to the ro - de - o.
D5
Ma - ma's on the front porch scream - in' out her warn - ing, "Girl, you'd
G5
bet - ter get your red head back in bed be - fore the morn - ing!
1.

2.
Chorus:
C5
cresc.
Ain't go - in' down 'til the
f
G5
Bb5
sun comes up. Ain't giv - in' in 'til they get e - nough.
C5
Go - ing 'round the world in a pick - up truck,
To Coda
1.
To Next Strain
2.
G5
N.C.
F5
F5
ain't go - in' down 'til the sun comes up. sun comes up.
mf

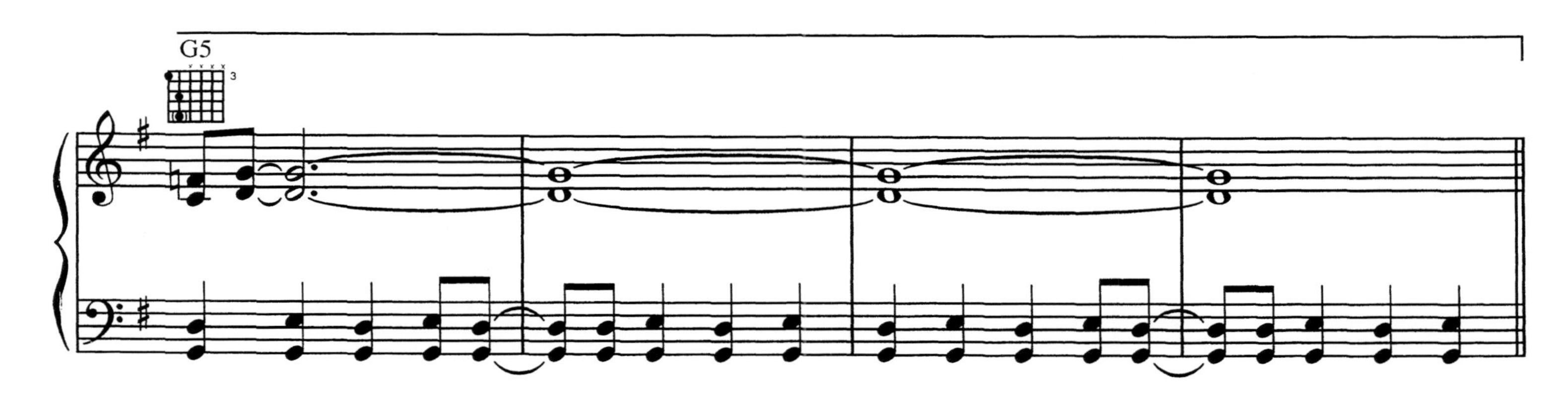
G5

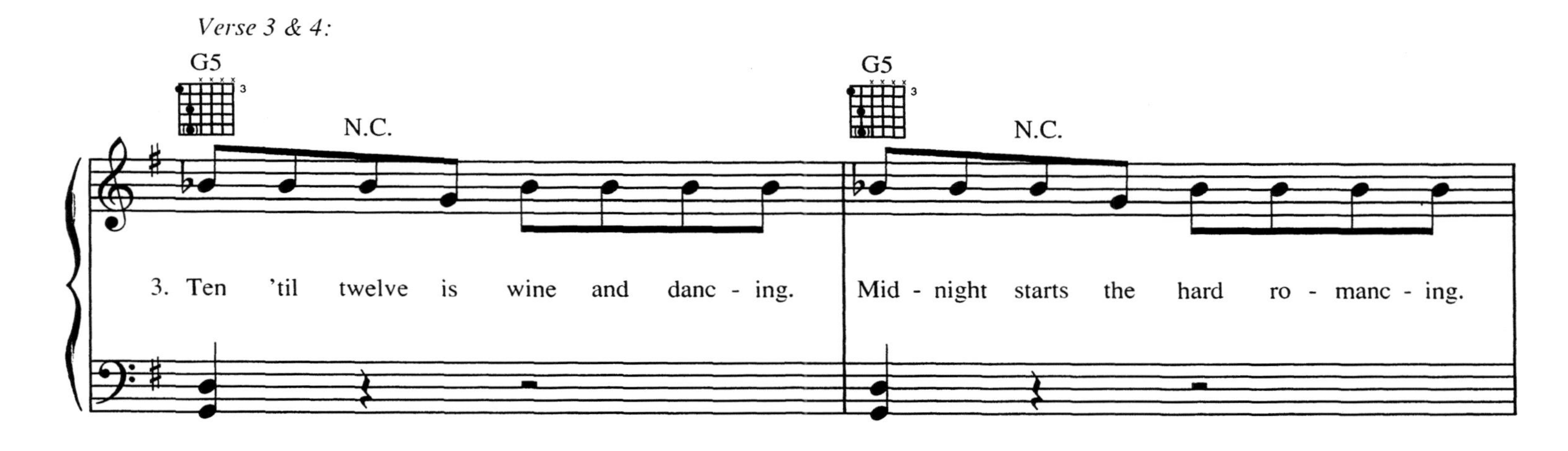
Verse 3 & 4:
G5
N.C.
G5
N.C.
3. Ten 'til twelve is wine and danc - ing.
Mid - night starts the hard ro - manc - ing.

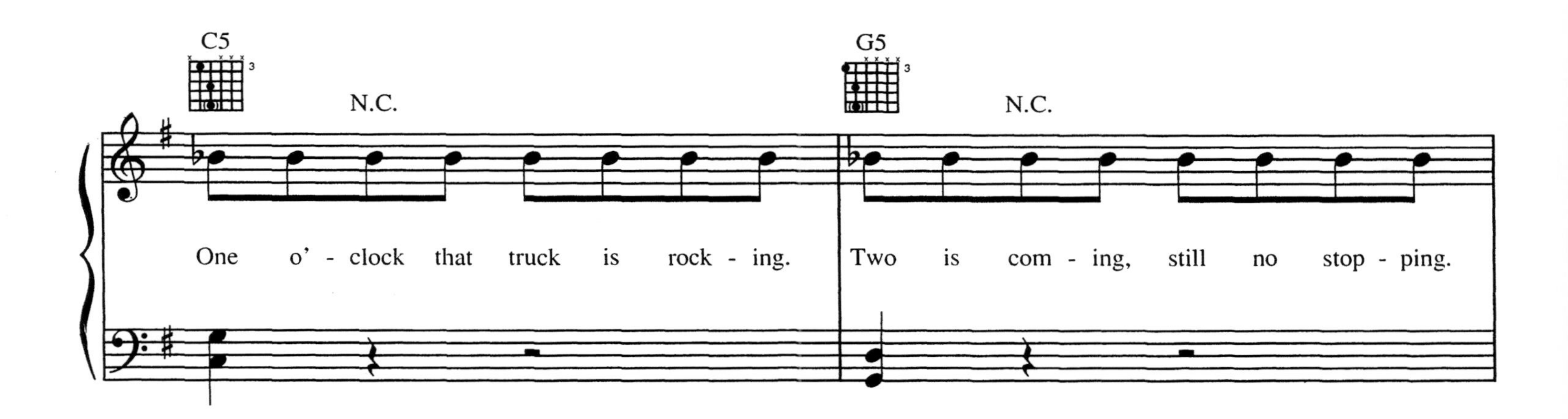
C5
N.C.
G5
N.C.
One o' - clock that truck is rock - ing.
Two is com - ing, still no stop - ping.

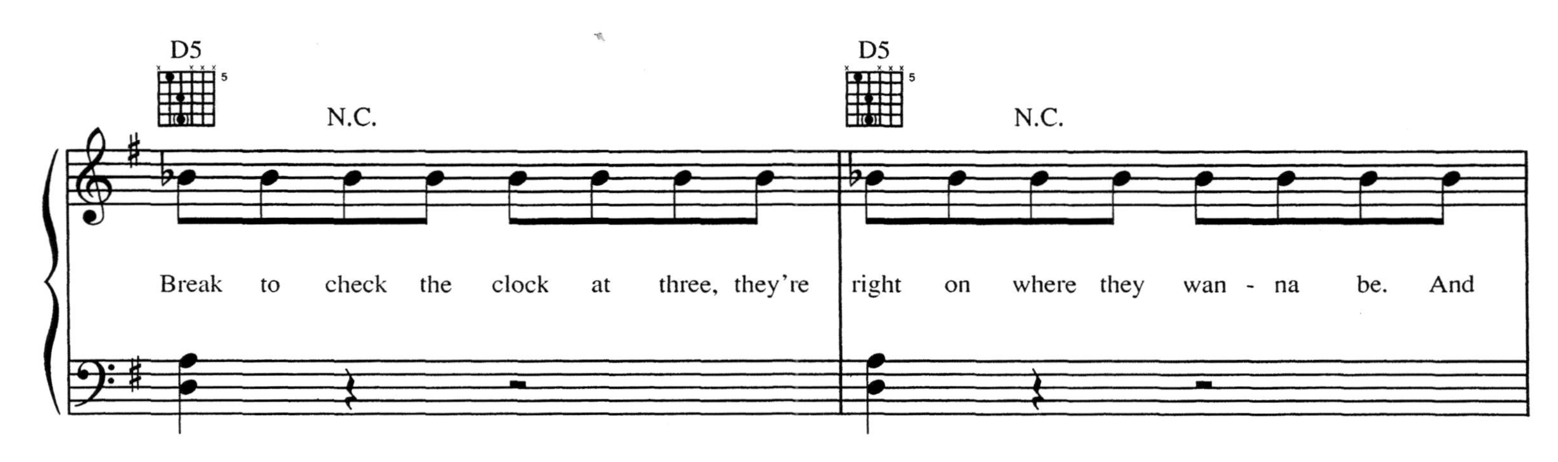
D5
N.C.
D5
N.C.
Break to check the clock at three, they're
right on where they wan - na be. And

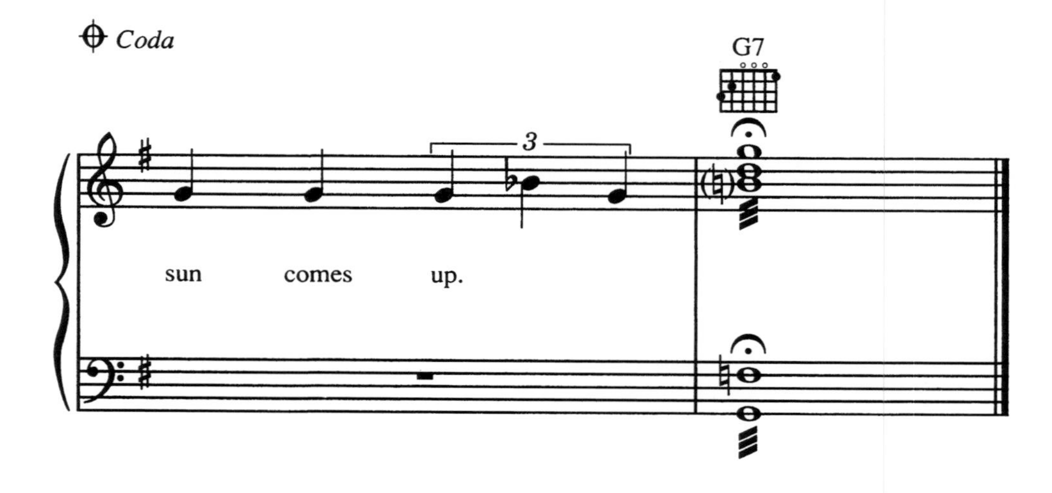

Verse 2:
Nine o'clock the show is ending,
But the fun is just beginning.
She knows he's anticipating
But she's gonna keep him waiting.
Grab a bite to eat
And then they're headin' to the honky tonk,
But loud crowds and line dancing
Just ain't what they really want.
Drive out to the boondocks and park down by the creek,
And where it's George Strait 'til real late
And dancing cheek to cheek.
(To Chorus:)

Verse 4:
Six o'clock on Saturday
Her folks don't know he's on his way.
The stalls are clean, the horses fed,
They say she's grounded 'til she's dead.
And here he comes around the bend,
Slowing down, she's jumping in.
Hey, Mom! Your daughter's gone
And there they go again. Hey!
(To Chorus:)

MORE THAN A MEMORY

Words and Music by
BILLY MONTANA, LEE BRICE
and KYLE JACOBS

Slow ballad ♩ = 69

Verse 1:

Guitar Capo 1 → F(9) C(9) C

Piano → G♭(9) D♭(9) D♭

People say she's only in my head.

mp

(with pedal)

More Than a Memory - 7 - 1
28974

Bb(9)
Bb
F
Cb(9)
Cb
Gb
But they don't re - al - ize is when you're
Chorus 1:
C
G/B
Db
Ab/C
dial-in' six num-bers just to hang up the phone, driv - in' 'cross town just to see if she's home,
Am
F
Bbm
Gb
wak-in' a friend in the dead of night just to hear him say, "It's gon-na be al - right." When you're find-
cresc.
C
G/B
Db
Ab/C
in' things to do not to fall a - sleep, 'cause you know she'll be there in your dreams,
mf

F
Gb
Dm
Ebm
C
Db
that's when she's more than a mem - o - ry.
Verse 2:
F(9)
Gb(9)
C(9)
Db(9)
C
Db
Took a match to ev - 'ry - thing she ev - er wrote.
Am7
Bbm7
Dm
Ebm
C/E
Db/F
Watched her words go up in smoke.
F(9)
Gb(9)
C(9)
Db(9)
C
Db
Tore all her pic - tures off the wall.

B♭
C♭
F/A
G♭/B♭
F
G♭
That ain't help - in' me at all, 'cause when you're
Chorus 2:
C
D♭
G/B
A♭/C
talk-in' out loud but no-bod-y's there, you look like hell and you just don't care,
Am
B♭m
F
G♭
drink-in' more than you ev-er drank, sink-in' down low-er than you ev-er sank. When you find
C
D♭
G/B
A♭/C
your-self fall-in' down up-on your knees, pray-in' to God, beg-gin' him "please," that's

F
Gb
Dm
Ebm
C
Db
when she's more than a mem - o - ry.
Bridge:
Bb
Cb
F
Gb
C
Db
She's more. She's
Bb
Cb
F/A
Gb/Bb
F
Gb
G
Ab
more. It's when you're
Chorus 3:
C
Db
G/B
Ab/C
dial-in' her num-ber just to hang up the phone, driv - in' 'cross town just to see if she's home,

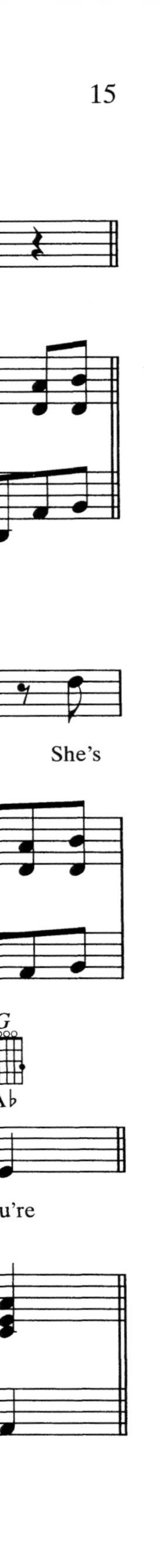

Am
B♭m
F
G♭ N.C.
wak-in' a friend in the dead of night just to hear him say, "It's gon-na be al - right." When you're find -
C
D♭
G/B
A♭/C
in' things to do not to fall a - sleep, 'cause you know she's wait-ing in your dreams,
F
G♭
Dm
E♭m
that's when she's more than a mem - o - ry.
C
D♭
G/B
A♭/C

Am
B♭m
F(9)
G♭(9)
decresc.
rit.
A little slower ♩ = 63
C(9)
D♭(9)
C
D♭
G/B
A♭/C
People say she's only in my head.
mp
Am7
B♭m7
It's gonna take time, but I'll forget.
rit.

AMERICAN HONKY-TONK BAR ASSOCIATION

Words and Music by
JIM RUSHING and BRYAN KENNEDY

C7
if you
need to pour your heart out
and

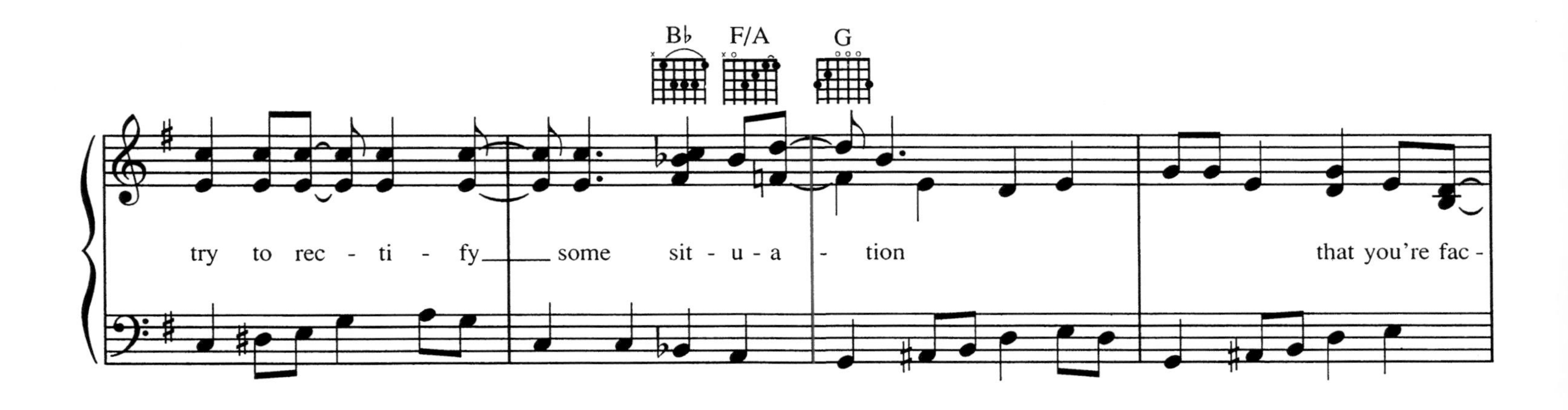
B♭ F/A G
try to rec - ti - fy some sit - u - a - tion
that you're fac -

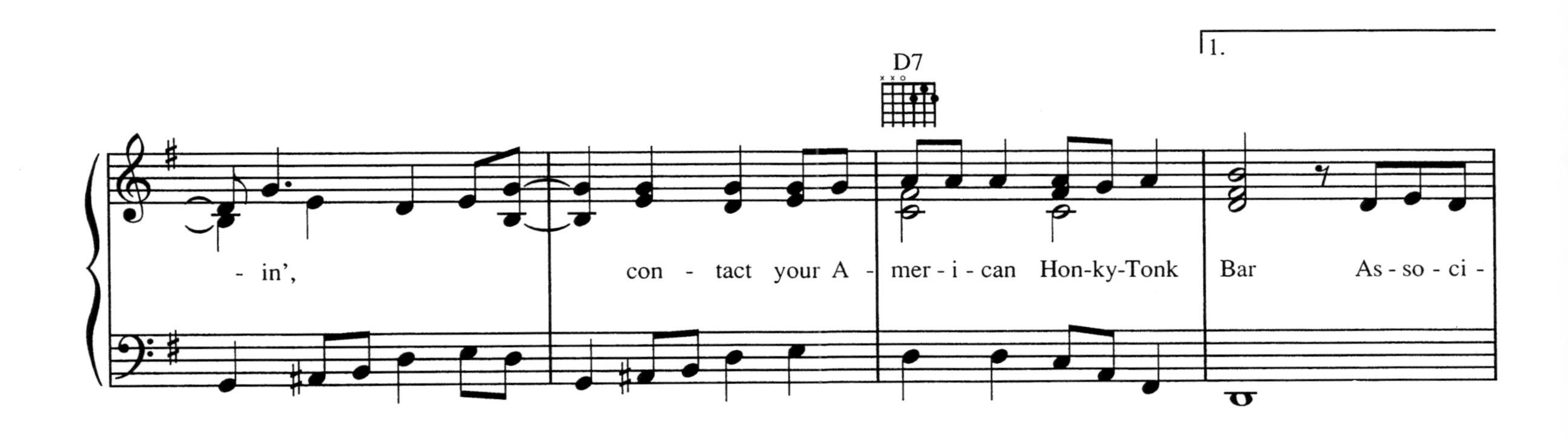
D7
1.
- in',
con - tact your A - mer - i - can Hon-ky-Tonk
Bar As - so - ci -

G7
a - tion.
2. When Un-cle

2.3.
G
G7
Bar As - so - ci - a - tion. It rep - re - sents the
Chorus:
C
hard hat, gun rack, ach - in' back, ov - er - taxed, flag - wav - in', fun - lov - in' crowd.
C7
G
G7
Their heart is in the mu - sic, and they love to play it loud.
D7
C
C♯
D
There's no forms or no ap - pli - ca - tions, there's no red tape ad-min - i - stra -

C
C♯
D7
G
To Coda
- tions; it's the A - mer - i - can Hon-ky-Tonk Bar As-so-ci - a-tion.
B♭
B
C
(Instrumental solo . . .
G
D7
G7
. . . end solo)

D.S. 𝄋 al Coda
3. We're
Coda
D7
Go join your A - mer - i - can Honk - y - Tonk Bar As - so - ci -
G7
a - tion.
Do not de - lay;
con - tact to - day

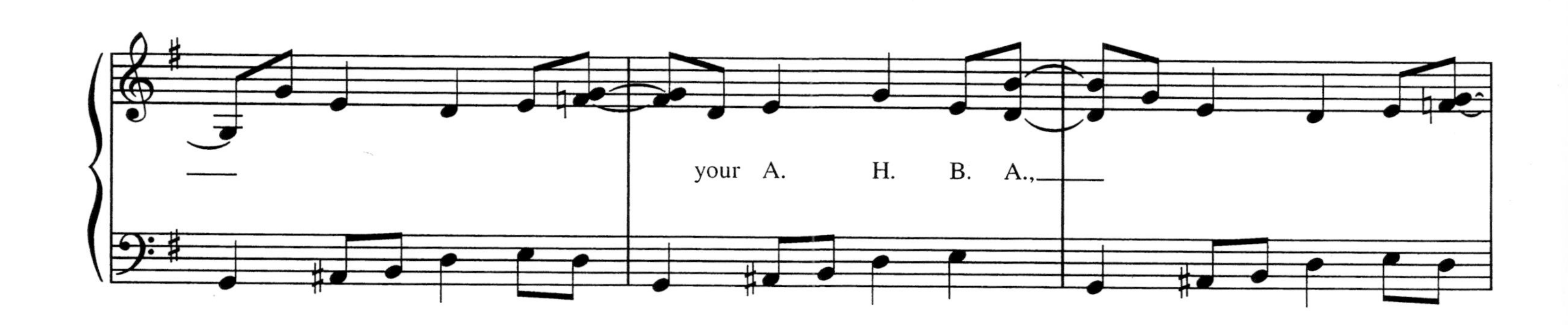

Verse 2:
When Uncle Sam dips in your pocket,
For most things you don't mind,
But when your dollar goes to all of those
Standing in a welfare line,
Rejoice, you have a voice,
If you're concerned about the destination
Of this great nation:
It's called the American Honky-Tonk Bar Association.
(To Chorus:)

Verse 3:
We're all one big family,
Throughout the cities and the towns.
We don't reach for handouts;
We reach for those who are down.
And every local chapter has a seven day a week
Available consultation
For your frustration.
It's called an American Honky-Tonk Bar Association.
(To Chorus:)

THE BEACHES OF CHEYENNE

Words and Music by
DAN ROBERTS, BRYAN KENNEDY
and GARTH BROOKS

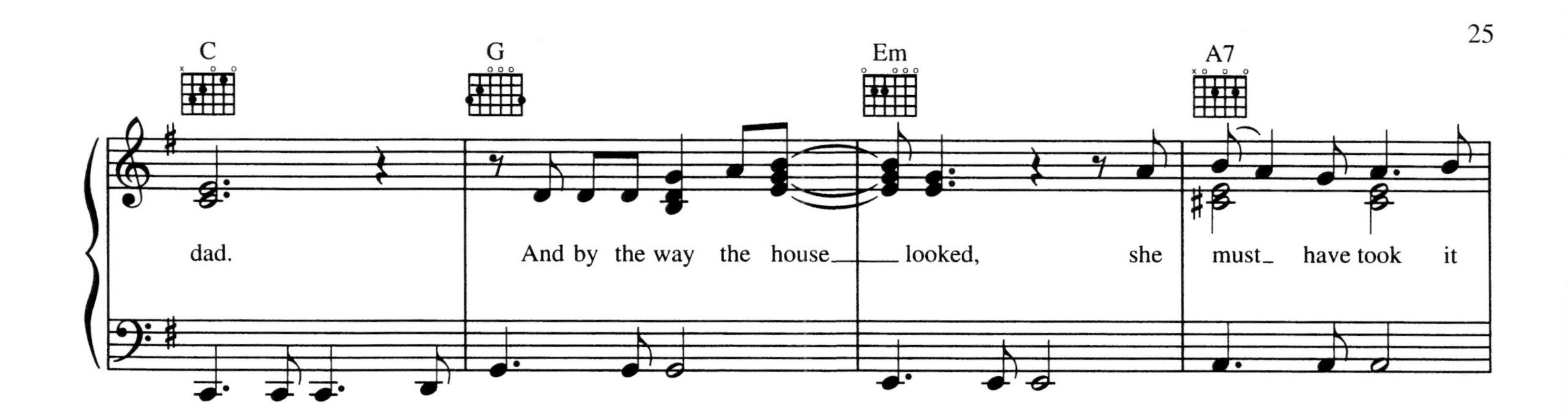
C
G
Em
A7
dad.
And by the way the house looked,
she
must_ have took it

D
G
C
G
bad.
The work-ers come_ on
Mon - day
to fix the

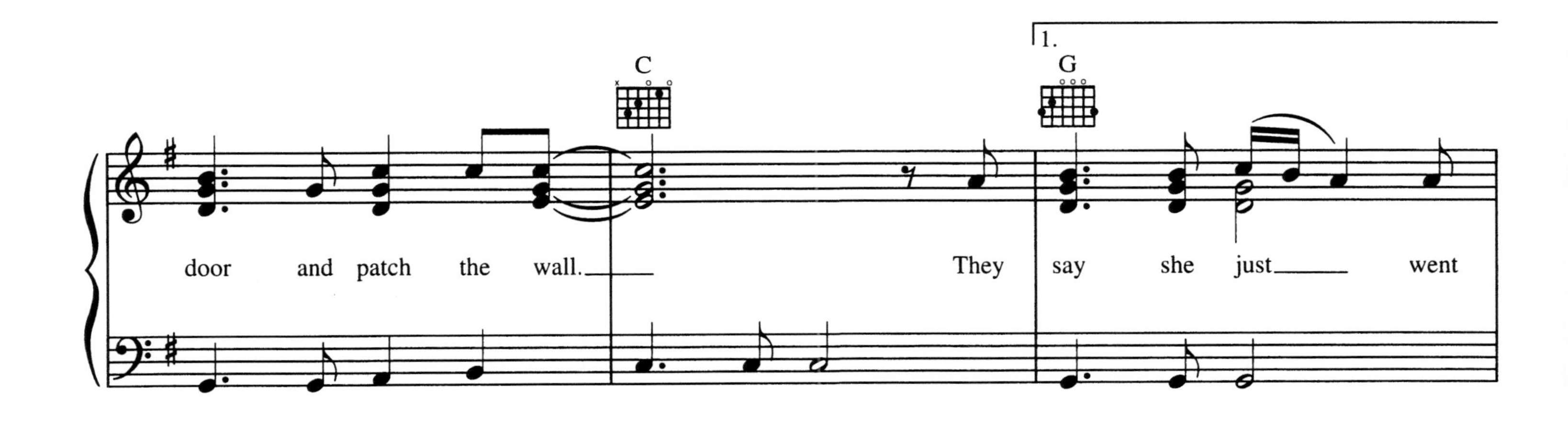
C
1.
G
door and patch the wall.
They
say she just went

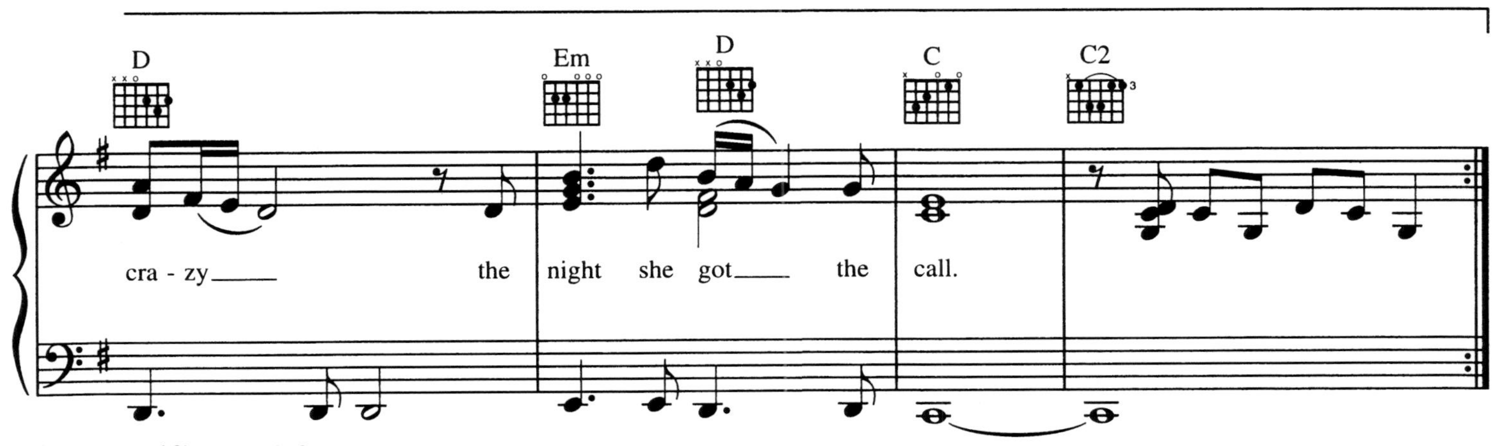
D
Em
D
C
C2
cra - zy
the
night she got the
call.

2.3.
Em
D
C
C2
died right there be - side him in Chey - enne.
cresc.
Chorus:
C
G
D
G
mf
1.2. They say she just went cra - zy,
3. See additional lyrics
scream-in' out his name. She ran
C
G
Em
D
C
out in - to the o - cean and to this day they claim that if you
G
F
C
G
go down by the wat-er, you'll see her foot-prints in the sand, 'cause ev-ery
D
C
1.
C2
D.S. 𝄋
night, she walks the beach-es of Chey - enne.

Verse 2:
Well, he was up in Wyoming,
And drew a bull no man could ride.
He promised her he'd turn out;
Well, it turned out that he lied.
And all their dreams that they'd been living
In the California sand
Died right there beside him
In Cheyenne.
(To Chorus 1:)

Verse 3:
They never found her body,
Just her diary by the bed.
It told about the fight they had,
And the words that she had said.
When he told her he was ridin',
She said, "Then I don't give a damn
If you never come back
From Cheyenne."
(To Chorus 2:)

Chorus 3:
Nobody can explain it;
Some say she's still alive.
They even claim they've seen her
On the shoreline late at night.
'Cause if you go down by the water,
You'll see her footprints in the sand,
'Cause every night, she walks the beaches
Of Cheyenne.
Yes, every night she walks the beaches
of Cheyenne.

BEER RUN
(B-double E-double Are You In?)

Words and Music by
KIM WILLIAMS, AMANDA WILLIAMS,
KEITH ANDERSON, GEORGE DUCAS
and KENT BLAZY

C
G
D
G
1. Twen-
Verse:
ty - five min - utes past quit - ting time___ sev - en of us crammed in - to that
2. 3. See additional lyrics
D
G
truck of mine,___ pay - ing no at - ten - tion to them high - way signs,___ do - ing
D
G
C
B
nine - ty miles an hour toward the coun - ty line.___ Quick sack, twelve pack,

B♭
A
To Coda
G
N.C.
back a - gain. It's a B double E double
1.
D
G
R U N.
2. My
2.
D
G
R U N.
Oh, I
Bridge:
B7
Em
can't stop think - ing what the hell they were drink - ing when they made this coun - ty dry.

B7
I got a week - long thirst and to make it worse, Lord,
C
C/D
it's my time to drive.
G
C
G
D
G
C

G
D
G
D.S. 𝄋 al Coda
3. Laugh -
Coda
G
N.C.
D
G
B double E double R U N.
N.C.
D
Hey! Like a B double E double R U
G
D
N.

Verse 2:
My buddies and their babies letting down their hair,
As long as we're together, it don't matter where.
Ain't got a lot of money but we just don't care,
Knowing half the fun is in the getting there.
Aztec, long necks, paychecks spent.
Oh, it's a B double E double R U N.
(To Bridge:)

Verse 3:
Laughing and bragging and a'carrying on,
We loaded up the wagons and we headed home.
I guess half a dozen cases doesn't last that long,
Come tomorrow morning it'll be all gone.
Then, it's turn around, leave town.
Sounds again like a B double E double R U N.
(To Coda)

CALLIN' BATON ROUGE

Words and Music by
DENNIS LINDE

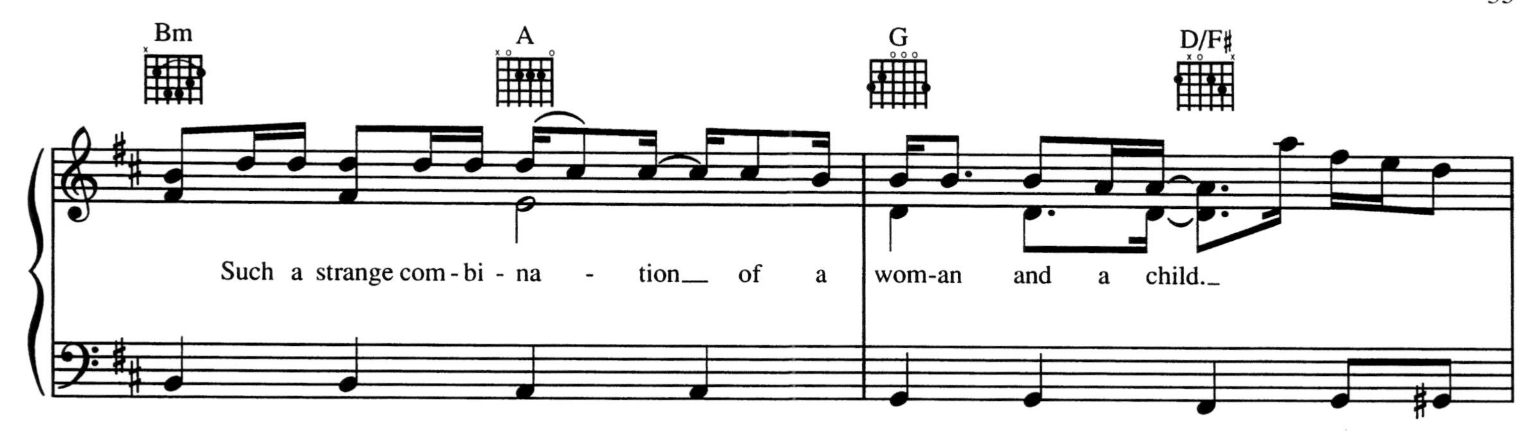
Bm
A
G
D/F♯
Such a strange com - bi - na - tion of a woman and a child.

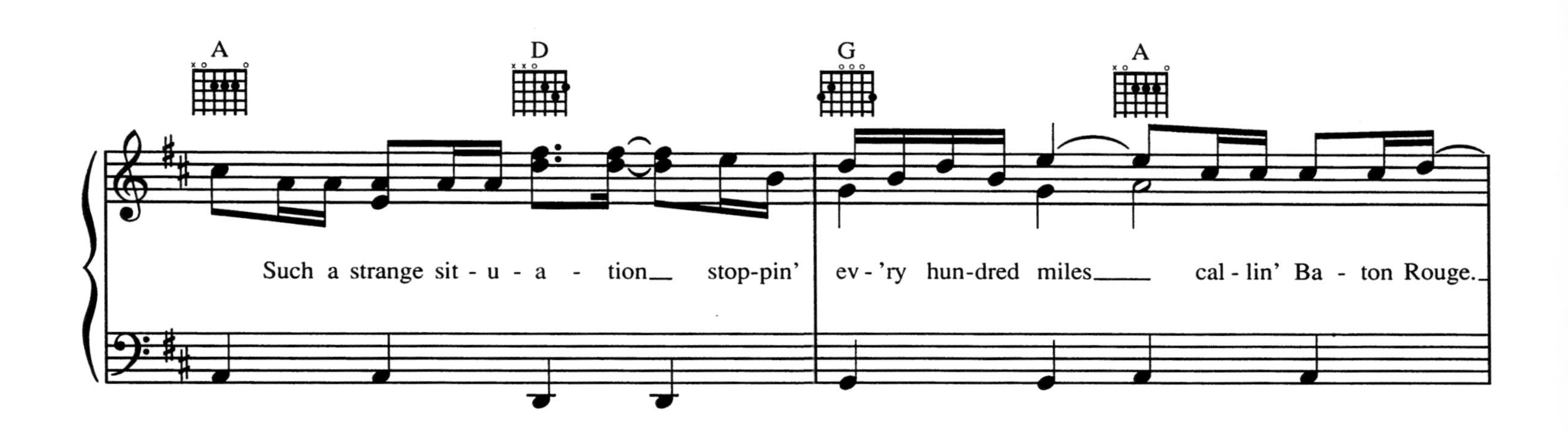
A
D
G
A
Such a strange sit - u - a - tion stop-pin' ev - 'ry hun-dred miles cal - lin' Ba - ton Rouge.

1.
D

2.
D
Chorus:
D
Op - er - a - tor, won't you put me on through? I got - ta send my love down to Ba - ton Rouge.
Hur - ry up; won't you put her on the line? I got - ta talk to the girl just - a one more time.
G
A
(Instrumental solo . . .
G

A
Bridge:
D
A/C♯
Hel-lo, Sa-man - tha dear, I hope
Bm
Asus
D
A/C♯
you're feel - in' fine.
And it won't be long un - til I'm
Bm
Asus
G
A
with you all the time, but un - til then
I'll spend my mon - ey up right down
D
G
A
to my last dime,
call - in' Ba - ton Rouge.

D
Op -
Chorus:
D
- er - a - tor, won't you put me on through? I got - ta send my love down to Ba - ton Rouge._ Hur -
- ry up; won't you put her on the line? I got - ta talk to the girl just - a one more time.___
G
A
Call - in' Ba - ton Rouge._

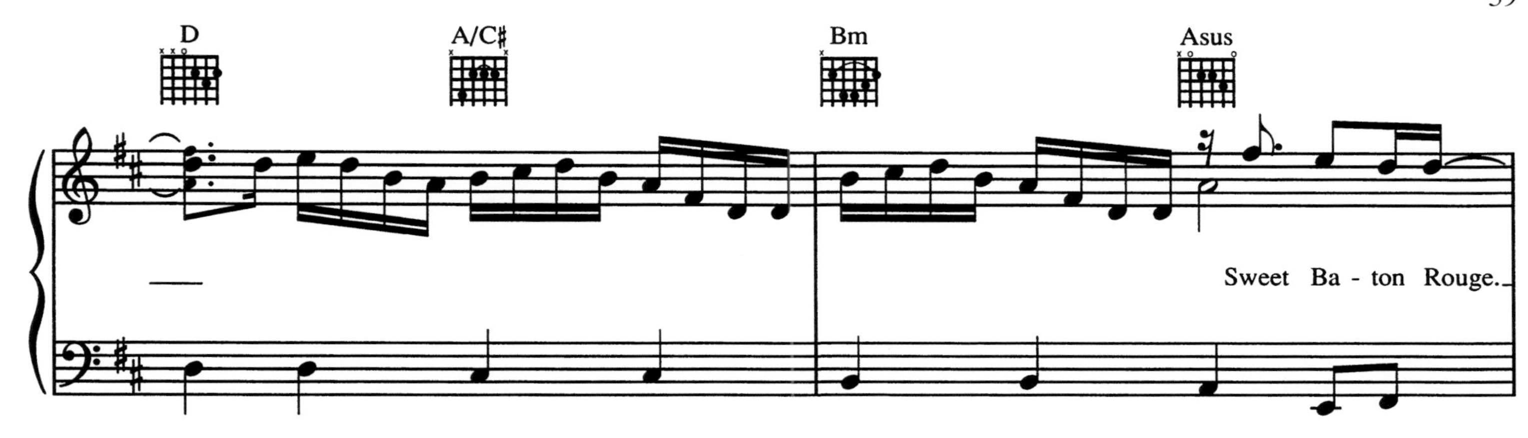

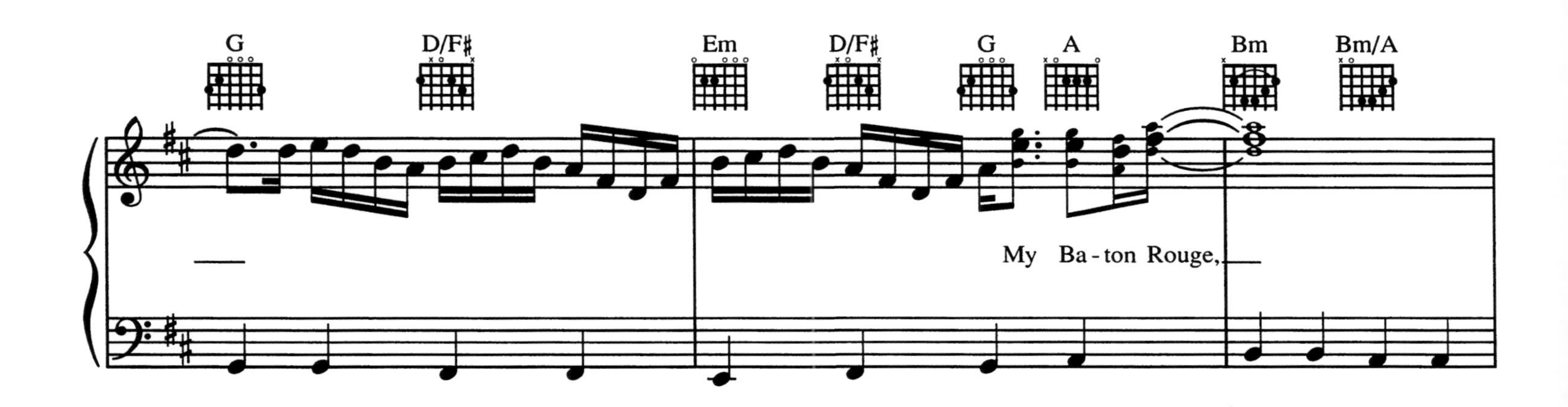

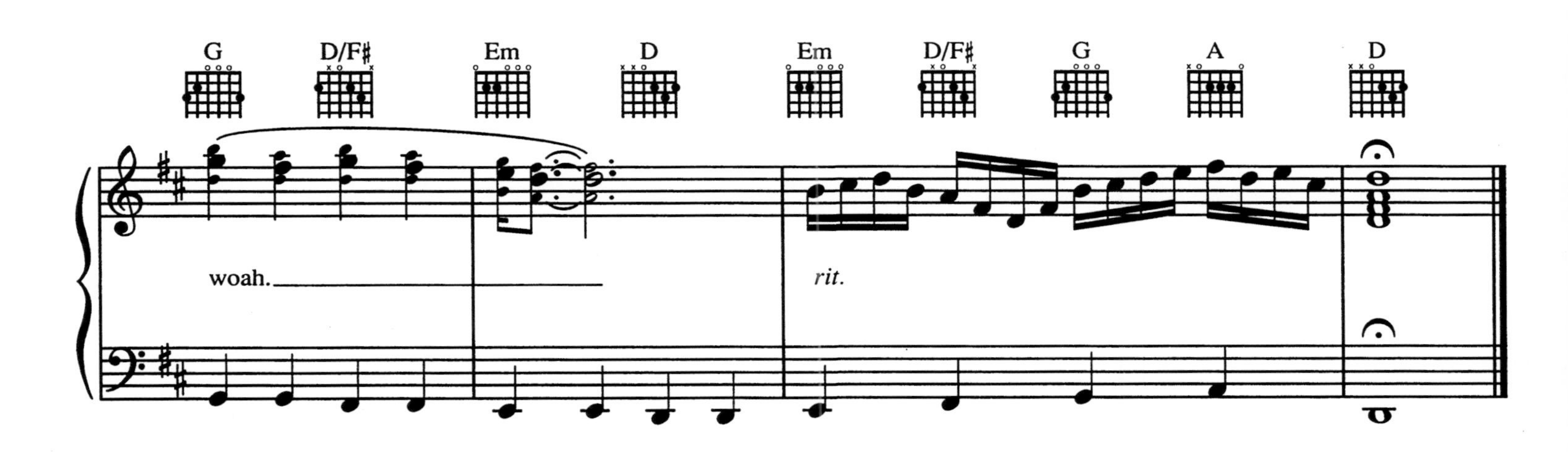

Verse 2:
A replay of last night's events
Roll through my mind,
Except a scene or two
Erased by sweet red wine.
And I see a truck stop sign ahead,
So I change lanes.
I need a cup of coffee,
And a couple dollars change,
Callin' Baton Rouge.
(To Chorus:)

THE CHANGE

Words and Music by
TONY ARATA and WAYNE TESTER

Slowly ♩ = 66

Ebmaj7 Gm Eb(9)

p

(with pedal)

Verse:

Dm7 F/Eb Eb Bb F/A

mp 1. One hand reach - es out and pulls a lost soul from harm,
2. See additional lyrics

Eb Eb/F F F/G Gm Ebmaj9

while a thou - sand more go un - spo - ken for. And they say,

Bb Ab

"What good have you done by sav - ing just this one? It's like

Fsus
F
whis - per - ing a prayer in the
fu - ry of a storm." And I hear them
cresc.
Chorus:
E♭maj9
B♭
say - ing, "You'll nev - er
change things, and no
mf
F7
E♭/B♭
mat - ter what you do, it's still the same
thing." But it's not the
Gm
E♭
world that I am
chang - ing, I
do this so this
E♭/F
world will know that it will not
change me.
1.
dim.

2.
Bridge:
Eb/Bb
Bb
Ab
cresc.
f
As long as one heart still holds on,
Gm7
Bb/F
F
Bb
then hope is nev-er real-ly gone.
And I hear them
Chorus 3:
Ebmaj9
Bb
say - ing, "You'll nev - er
change things, and no
f
F7
Eb/Bb
Bb
mat - ter what you do it's still the same
thing." But it's not the

Verse 2:
This heart still believes
That love and mercy still exist.
While all the hatreds rage, and so many say
That love is all but pointless in madness such as this;
It's like trying to stop a fire with the moisture from a kiss.
(To Chorus:)

THE DANCE

Words and Music by
TONY ARATA

C
D
was right.
would fall.
How could I
Hey, who's
have known
to say?
that you'd ev - er
You know I might
cresc.
Em
D/F♯
Chorus:
say good - bye?
have changed it all.
And now,
mf
I'm glad I did - n't know
Bm7
the way it all would end,
the way it all would go.
Our lives
are bet-ter left to chance.
I could have missed the pain,
but I'd have had to miss
1.
G
C/G G
C/G G D/G C/G G
D.S.
the
dance.
dim.
2. Hold-ing you,
mp

2.
G
C
D
dance.
Yes, _ my life, ___
it's bet-ter left _ to _ chance. ___
I could have missed _ the pain, _
Bm7
C
D
N.C.
___ but I'd have had _ to _ miss ___
the ___
dance.
rit.
a tempo
mp
Em
C
Dsus
D
8va
Em7(4)
Repeat ad lib. and fade

Garth Brooks with Huey Lewis

WORKIN' FOR A LIVIN'

Words and Music by
HUEY LEWIS and CHRIS HAYES

Verses 1 & 2:

work - ing here for - ev - er, at least un - til I die.
hit - ting up my bud - dy's got me feel - ing like a jerk.
Damned if you do, damned if you don't. I'm
Car pay - ment, in - sur - ance, al - i - mo - ny, rent; I
s'pposed to get a raise next week, you know damn well I won't.
get a check on Fri - day, but it's al - read - y spent.
D9
Work -
Chorus:
A7
in' for a liv - in'. (Work - in'.) Work - in' for a liv - in'. (Work-

G
D7
in'.)
Work-in' for a liv-in', liv - in' and a-work-in'. I'm
A7
N.C.
1.
A7
tak-ing what they're giv-in' 'cause I'm work-in' for a liv-in'.
2.
Bridge:
G
D
G
D
work-in' for a liv-in'. Ah, work-in' for a liv-in'.

G
D
G
D
G
D
Ah,
tak - ing what they're giv - in'.
Ah,
G
D
G
D
E
work-in' for a liv - in'.
Ah,
ah.
A7
(Harmonica solo ad lib....

G
D
A5
Verse 3:
A7
GARTH:
3. Bus - boy, bar - tend - er, la - dies of the night,
...end solo)
G5
A7
HUEY:
grease mon-key, ex - junk - ie, win - ner of the fight, walk - ing on the streets it's

real - ly all the same. NAS - CAR, rock - star, an - y oth - er day. Work -
Chorus:
D9
A7
in' for a liv - in'. (Work - in'.) I'm work - in' for a liv - in'. (Work -
G
D7
in'.) I'm work - in' for a liv - in', liv - in' and a - work - in'. I'm
A7
tak - ing what they're giv - in' 'cause I'm work - in' for a liv - in'.

G
D7
A7
GARTH:
Work - in' for a liv - in', liv - in' and a - work - in'.
(Instrumental ad libs. and drum fills)
sfz

THE FEVER

Words and Music by
STEVEN TYLER, JOE PERRY,
BRYCE KENNEDY and DAN ROBERTS

Driving rock ♩=184

A5 G5 A5

f

(Instrumental solo ad lib...

...end solo)

1. He's got a

Verses 1 & 2:

A5

split fin - ger wrap,_ and his rope's pulled way too tight._____
one last breath_ and time turns in - side out;_____

He's got a lu - na - tic smile__ 'cause he's real - ly drawn deep_ to - night._____
then the gate busts o - pen to the world he dreams_ a - bout._____

1. He's got a
2. He's got a

Chorus 1 & 2:
A
D
fe - ver,
fe - ver,
fe - ver,
fe - ver,
A
D
fe - ver,
fe - ver,
fe - ver.
fe - ver.
Grab
Stick
A
E
A
a hold of an - y - thing and hold on tight; it hits you like the ven - om from a
a rope on an - y - thing, 'cause he don't care; he'd e - ven take a ride in an e -
D
A
E
A5
G5
rat - tle - snake bite. We're all here 'cause he's not all there to - night.
lec - tric chair. We're all here 'cause he's not all there to - night.

1.
A5
(Inst. solo ad lib...
...end solo) 2. He takes
2.
A5
Bm
Cdim
A/C♯
He says, "It's
Bridge:
D
A
real - ly kind - a sim - ple: keep your mind in the mid - dle while your butt spins 'round and 'round.
D
Take heed to Sank-ey's preach-in', keep a - lift - in' and a - reach-in' and a -

E
A5
rid - in' like there ain't no clowns."
(Inst. solo ad lib...
D
E
3. What he
...end solo)

Verse 3:
A5
loves might kill him, but he's got no choice; he's a dif - f'rent breed with a
voice down deep in - side that's scream - in' he was born to ride.
Chorus 3:
A
D
3. He's got a fe - ver, fe - ver,
A
D
fe - ver, fe - ver.
A
E
Fe - ver makes you cra - zy, 'cause it makes no sense; like

A
D
A
run - nin' from your shad - ow out of
self de - fense._ But
he won't run,_ and ba - by,

E
A
D
he can't hide;_ he
thinks the odds are e - ven leav - in'
one hand tied._ He

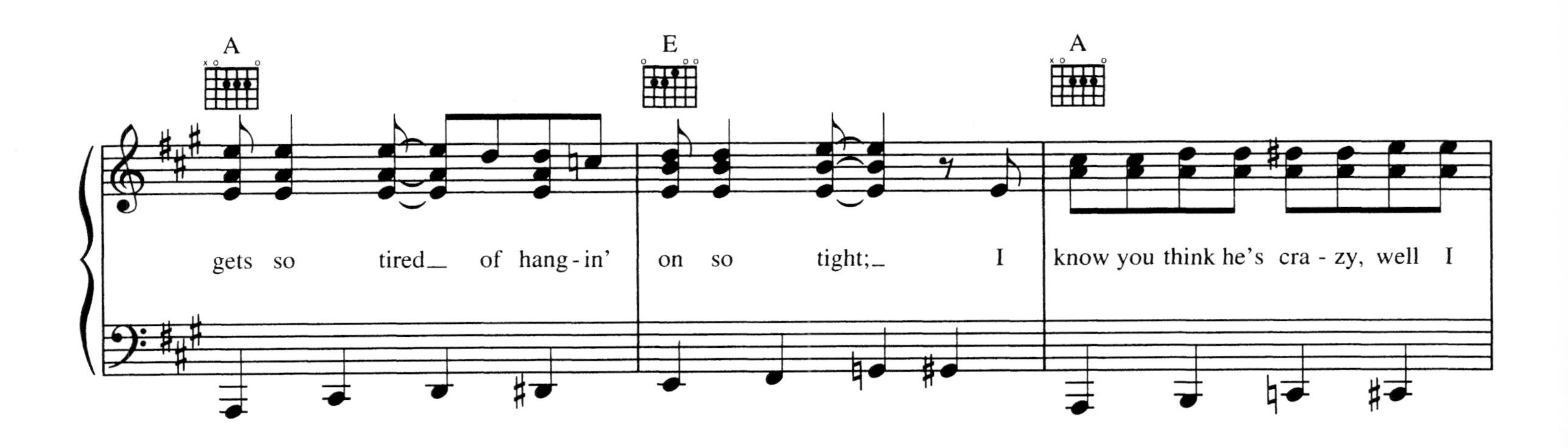
A
E
A
gets so tired_ of hang - in'
on so tight;_ I
know you think he's cra - zy, well I

D
A
E
A
think you're right._
We're all here_ 'cause he's
not all there,_ that's right!

FRIENDS IN LOW PLACES

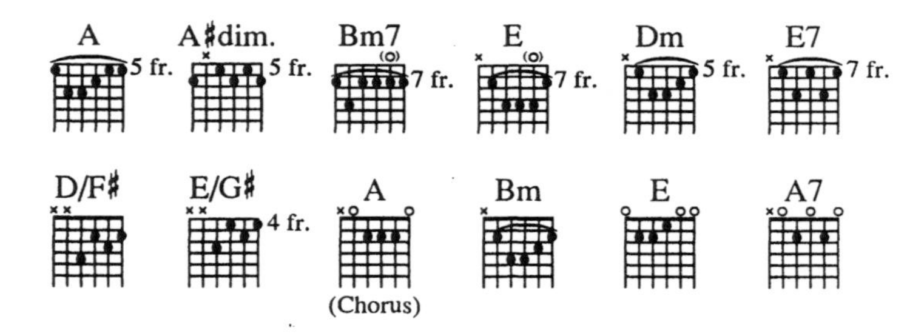

Words and Music by
DEWAYNE BLACKWELL
and EARL BUD LEE

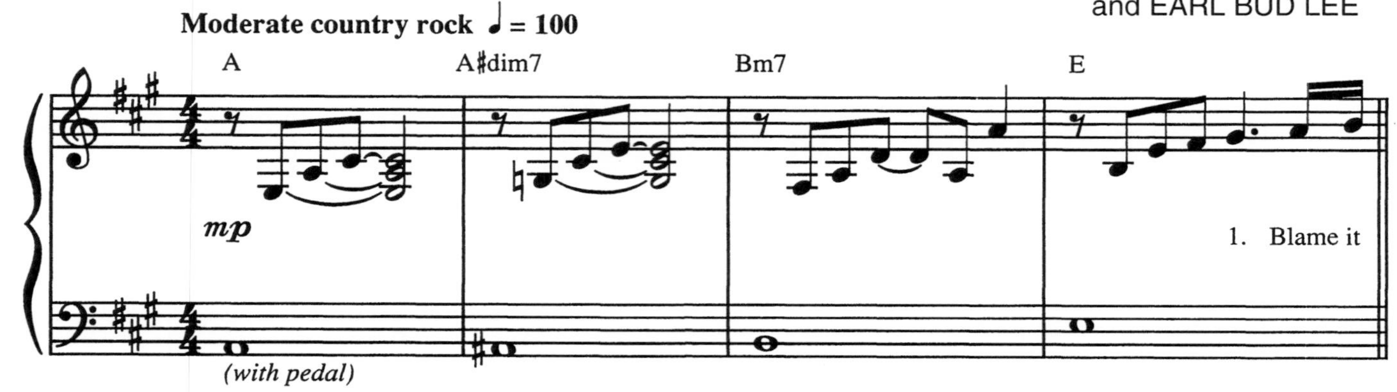

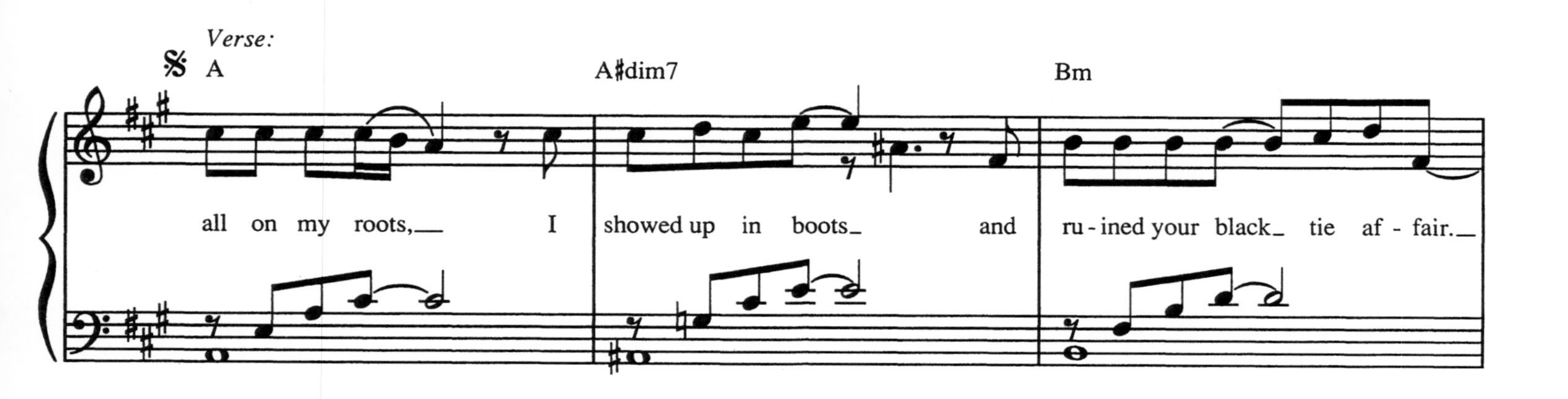

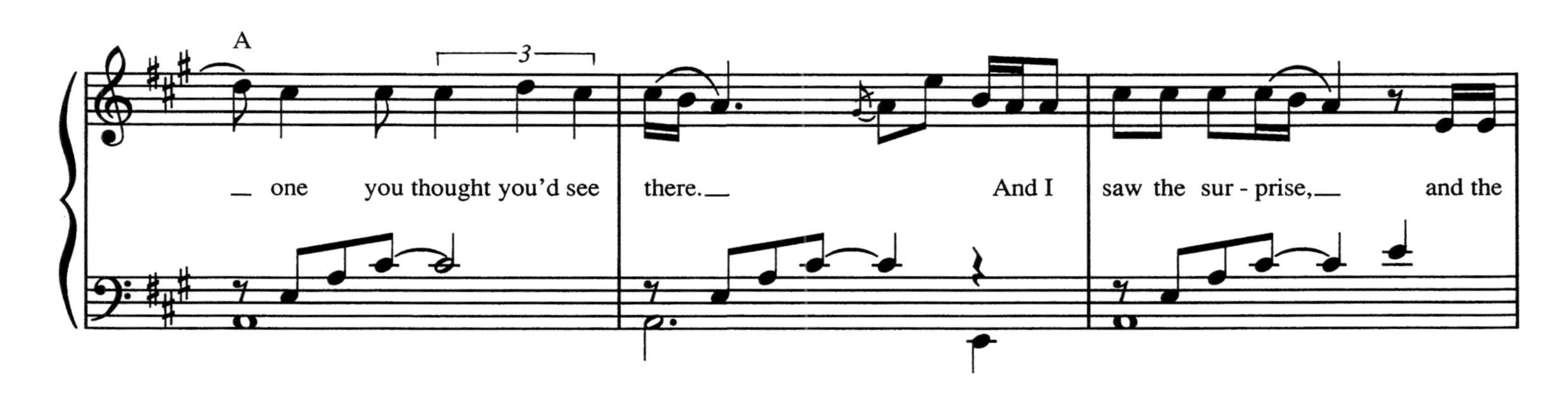
A
3
one you thought you'd see there. And I saw the sur - prise, and the

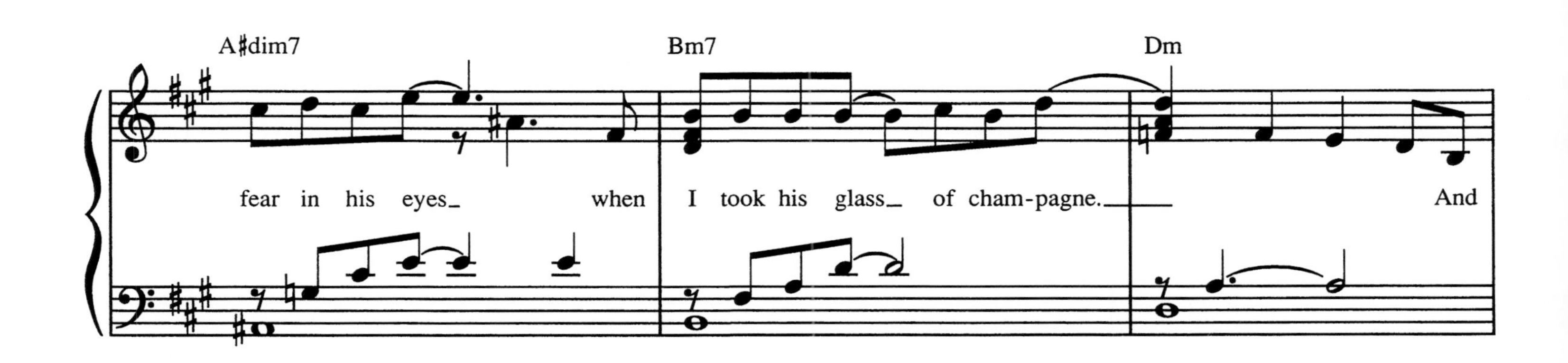
A♯dim7
Bm7
Dm
fear in his eyes when I took his glass of cham-pagne. And

E7
I toast-ed you, said hon - ey, we may be through, but you'll nev - er hear me com - plain.
cresc. poco a poco

D/F♯
E/G♯
Chorus:
A
'Cause I've got friends in low plac - es where the
f

Verse 2:
Well, I guess I was wrong.
I just don't belong.
But then, I've been there before.
Everything's all right.
I'll just say goodnight,
And I'll show myself to the door.
Hey, I didn't mean
To cause a big scene.
Just give me an hour and then,
Well, I'll be as high
As that ivory tower
That you're livin' in.
(To Chorus:)

MIDNIGHT SUN

Words and Music by
JERROD NIEMANN, RICHIE BROWN
and GARTH BROOKS

Slowly, freely

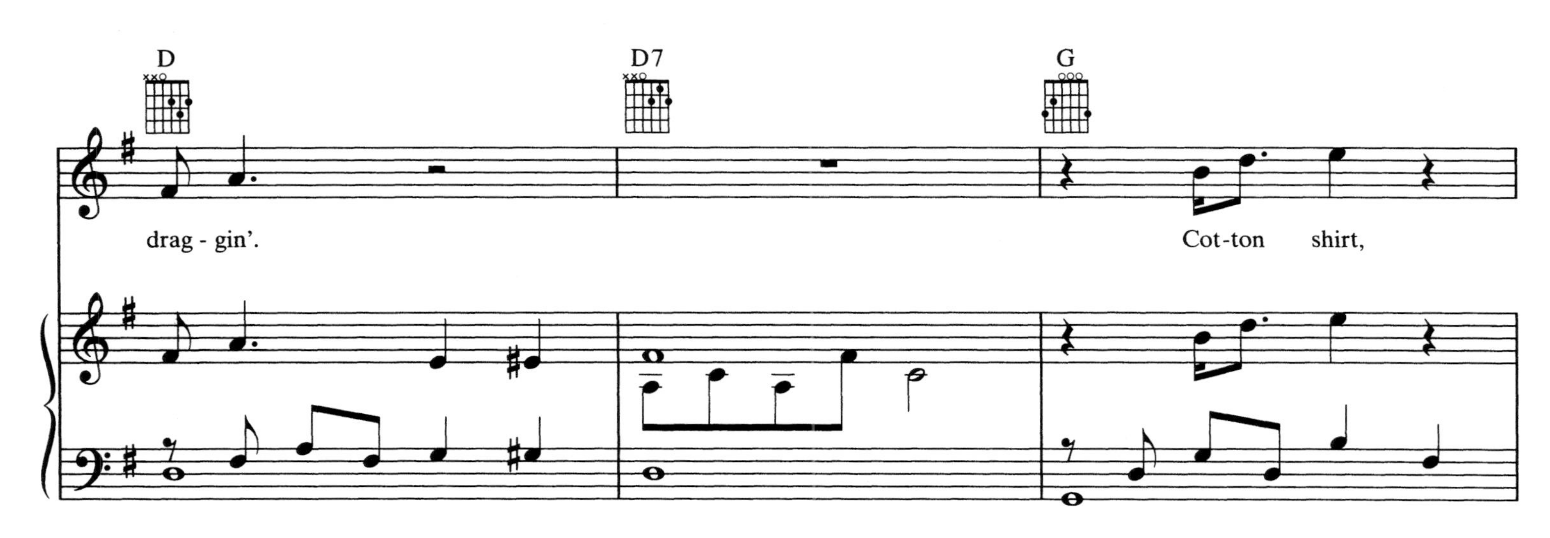

Midnight Sun - 7 - 1
28974

G7
C
C7
cot - ton-mouth,
cold ones wait - in'
at the house.
G
D7
N.C.
It's time for me to get down off the wag - on.
Moderate country shuffle (♩ = 120)
Chorus 1:
G
N.C.
C
Hose me down and dress me up,
fire up that old
pick - up truck.
G
Out the gate and let them hors - es run.
f

D
D7
G
Juke - box and
G7
C
swing - ing doors,
soft and pret - ties on a hard - wood floor.
G
D
A cow - boy's work just ain't nev - er done
C
G/B
Am
D
in the land of the mid - night

G
Am
sun.
D7
G
dim.
Verses 2 & 3:
D
G
2. Find a look-er, have her hold my keys, and tell her lat-er we'll be
3. Shoot the breeze while shoot-in' pool and still you're sweat-in' like a
mf
D
need-in' these. Grab a cold one, turn it up-side down, to that
rent-ed mule. Get-tin' loud with all my cow-boy friends, the

Chorus 2 & 3:
C
D
G
N.C.
hon - ky - tonk - in' sound.
par - ty nev - er ends.
So hose me down and
cresc.
f
C
dress me up,
fire up that old pick - up truck.
G
D
Out the gate and let them hors - es run.
D7
'Cause eight o' - clock comes twice a day
Look - y there who waits for me,

G
and ei - ther way you'll find me chas - in' strays.
smil - in' sweet - ly, hold - in' up my keys.
A cow-boy's work
D
just ain't nev - er done
C
G/B
in the
Am
D
G
land of the mid - night sun.
1.
Am
D7

G
2.
C
G/B
In the
dim.

Am
D
C
land
of the mid - night
sun.

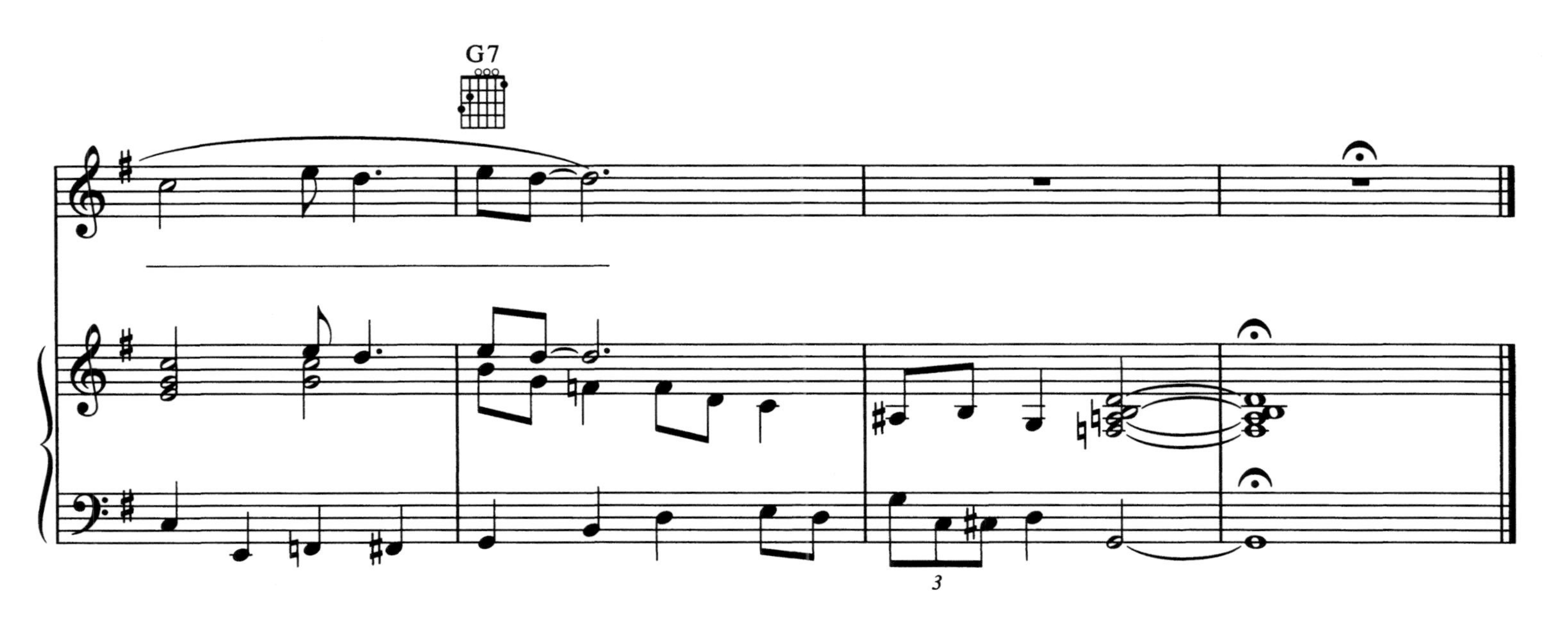
G7

GOOD RIDE COWBOY

Words and Music by
BRYAN KENNEDY, JERROD LEE NIEMANN,
RICHIE BROWN and BOB DOYLE

E7
A7
D7
cow-boy hat and that Co - pen - ha - gen smile. And from buck-ing broncs to
G7
E7
hon - ky - tonks, he al - ways sang a cow-boy's song. We were
D
B7
E7
A7
D
much too young, hav-ing too much fun, as we all sang a - long. And we sang,
Chorus:
G7
D7
G7
life's a high - way, there's on - ly one way you're gon - na get

D7 G7 D B7
through__ it. When she starts to twist,__ be more like Chris,__ pull your
E7 A N.C. D7
hat down tight____ and just Le - Doux it. When that whis - tle blows__ and that
G7 F#7 F7 E7
crowd ex - plodes,__ and them pick - up men are at your side,____ they tell you,
D A7 D
good ride,____ cow - boy,__ good ride.________

A
D
B7
2. From gold_
Verse 2:
E7
A7
__ buck-les to__ gold rec - ords,__ well, once a-gain, he was spin-ning 'round._
E7
F♯7
__ He took the whole world on,__ and he turned us on__ to that west-ern un-der-ground._
B7
E7
__ And from "Bare-back Jack"_ to "This Cow-boy's Hat,"__ the songs_

A7
F#7
E
were strong-er than his pain.
He would not slow down,
from
C#7
F#7
B7
E7
town to town, like chil-dren run-ning through the rain.
And we sang,
Chorus:
A7
E7
A7
E7
life's a high-way, there's on-ly one way you're gon-na get through it.
When she
A7
E
C#7
F#7
starts to twist, be more like Chris, pull your hat down tight and

B
N.C.
E7
just Le - Doux it. When that whis - tle blows_ and that crowd ex - plodes,_ and them
A7
G♯7
G7
F♯7
E7
pick - up men are at your side,_ they tell you, good ride,_ cow -
1.
B7
E
boy,_ good ride._ And we sang,
2.
B7
E
boy,_ good_ ride._ I bet he crossed_

D
A7
G#7
G7
F#7
that riv - er Jor - dan, with Saint Pe - ter on the oth - er side
E
B7
sing-in', good ride, cow - boy, good ride.
E
A
E
He sang, good ride, cow -
B7
E
boy, good ride.

IF TOMORROW NEVER COMES

Words and Music by
KENT BLAZY and GARTH BROOKS

D
Am7
D
C
would she ever doubt the way I feel about her in my
G
C/G
G
Chorus:
C
heart. If to-mor-row nev-er comes, will she know how much I
G
D
Am7
loved her? Did I try in ev-ery way to show her ev-ery-day
D
C
G
Am7
G/B
that she's my on-ly one? And if my time on earth were
C
D
Em7
Bm7
through, and she must face this world with-out me,

Verse 2:
'Cause I've lost loved ones in my life.
Who never knew how much I loved them.
Now I live with the regret
That my true feelings for them never were revealed.
So I made a promise to myself
To say each day how much she means to me
And avoid that circumstance
Where there's no second chance to tell her how I feel. ('Cause)
(To Chorus:)

IN ANOTHER'S EYES

Words and Music by
BOBBY WOOD, JOHN PEPPARD
and GARTH BROOKS

G
1.
D
A7sus
2.
D
Em7
D/F♯
oth-er's eyes, yeah, yeah. 2. In an- In an-
Chorus:
G
D/F♯
A7sus
A7
oth-er's eyes, I'm a-fraid that I can't see this pic-ture per-fect por-trait that they paint
D
G
Bm7
of me. They don't re-al-ize, and I pray they nev-er do. 'Cause ev-
Em7
D/F♯
A7sus
A7
To Coda
'ry time I look, I'm see-in' you in an-

Verse 3:
G/D D C/G G D
oth-er's eyes. Whoa. 3. In an-oth-er's eyes, star-in'
A7sus A7 D G
back at me, I see a sink-ing soul try-ing des-p'rate-ly to turn the tide
D A7sus A7 G
be-fore it dies in an-oth-er's eyes, yeah,
Bridge:
D Bm A/C♯ D Em7 D/F♯ G
yeah. And what they don't see, Lord, is kill-ing me. It's a

Verse 2:
In another's eyes, I can do no wrong.
He believes in me and his faith is strong.
I'd never fall or even compromise,
In another's eyes.
(To Chorus:)

LEARNING TO LIVE AGAIN

Words and Music by
DON SCHLITZ and
STEPHANIE DAVIS

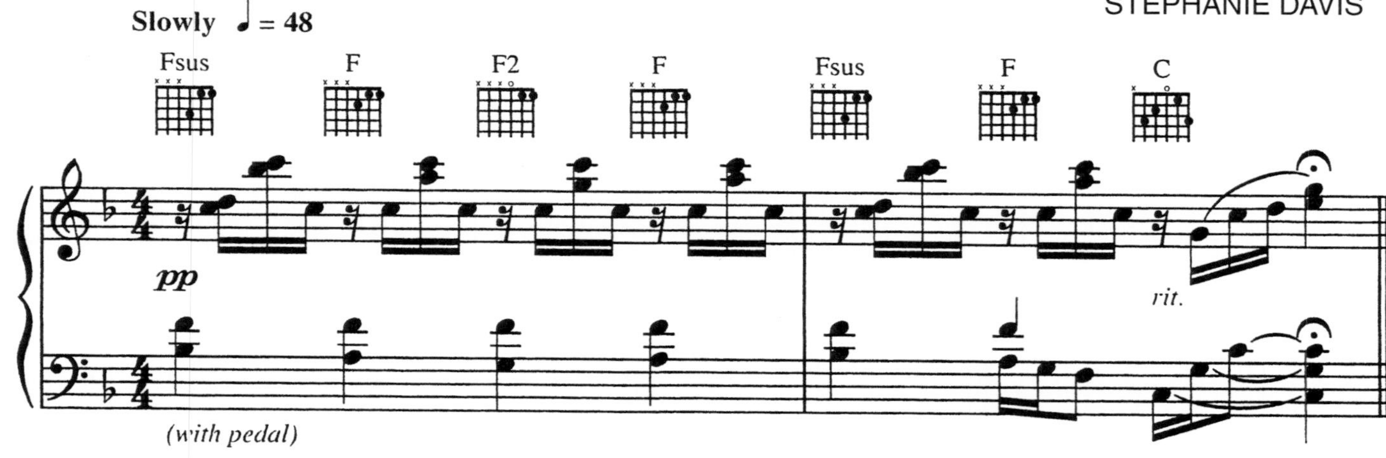

2. 4. 5.
Chorus:
Dm C B♭ F
here I go a - gain. 1. I'm gon-na smile my best smile, and I'm gon-na laugh
cresc.
mf
C F B♭ Am
like it's go - in' out of style, look in - to her eyes and pray that she don't see
B♭ C Gm F/A B♭ C
that learn-ing to live a - gain is kill-ing me.
1.
D.S. 𝄋
Fsus F F2 F Fsus F C
p

Verse 3:
Little cafe, table for four,
But there's just conversation for three.
I like the way she let me get the door;
I wonder what she thinks of me.

Verse 4:
Debbie just whispered, "You're doing fine."
And I wish that I felt the same.
She's asked me to dance; now her hand's in mine;
Oh my God, I've forgotten her name. *(To Chorus:)*

Verse 5:
Now here we are beneath her porch light,
And I say what a great time it's been;
A kiss on the cheek, a whisper goodnight,
And I say, "Can I see you again?"

Chorus 3:
And she just smiles her best smile,
And she laughs like it's goin' out of style,
Looks into my eyes, and says, "We'll see."
Oh, this learning to live again is killing me.
God, this learning to live again is killing me.

Chorus 2:
But I'm gonna smile my best smile,
And I'm gonna laugh like it's going out of style,
Look into her eyes, and pray that she don't see
This learning to live again is killing me.

PAPA LOVED MAMA

Words and Music by
KIM WILLIAMS and GARTH BROOKS

B7
part she could - n't han - dle was the be - ing a - lone, I guess she
C
B7
E7
need-ed more to hold than just a tel - e - phone. Pa - pa called Ma - ma each and
A7
ev - ery night, just to ask her how she was and if us kids were al - right. Ma-
B7
C
- ma would wait for that call to come in but when Dad - dy'd hang up, she was

B7
E7
gone a - gain.
1.3. Ma-
cresc.
f
Chorus:
A7
E7
- ma was a look-er, Lord, how she shined. Pa - pa was a good-'n but the
A7
jeal-ous kind. Pa - pa loved ma-ma, ma - ma loved men.
To Coda
1.
E5
N.C.
B5
E7
Ma-ma's in the grave-yard, Pa - pa's in the pen.
dim.

mf
2. Well, it was
2.
E5
N.C.
B5
E7
D.S. 𝄋 al Coda
hit the brakes and he was
shift - ing gears.
Ma -
Coda
E5
N.C.
B5
E7
Ma-ma's in the grave - yard, Pa
- pa's in the
pen.

Verse 2:
Well, it was bound to happen and one night it did,
Papa came home and it was just us kids.
He had a dozen roses and a bottle of wine,
If he was lookin' to surprise us, he was doin' fine.
I heard him cry for Mama up and down the hall,
Then I heard a bottle break against the bedroom wall.
That old diesel engine made an eerie sound,
When papa fired it up and headed into town.

Chorus 2:
Well, the picture in the paper showed the scene real well,
Papa's rig was buried in the local motel.
The desk clerk said he saw it all real clear.
He never hit the brakes and he was shifting gears.
(To Chorus 1:)

LONGNECK BOTTLE

Words and Music by
STEVE WARINER and RICK CARNES

* Cue notes represent vocal harmonies.

Longneck Bottle - 4 - 1
28974

D
G
me, you know she won't un - der - stand. Long - neck
D
A
D
bot-tle, let go of my hand.
1. Hey, bar -
...end solo)
Verse:
G
D
room mir-ror on the wall, go stare at some - one else.
2. See additional lyrics
E♭
E
Don't show the world the fool I am, just
A
keep it to your - self. Long - neck

Chorus:
D
G
D
bot - tle,
let go of my
hand.
G
Whoa, juke - box, don't start
play - ing that song a - gain,
D
G
'cause there's a
girl at home who loves
me, you know
D
G
she won't un - der - stand.
Long - neck
D
A
1.
D
bot - tle,
let go of my
hand.

Instrumental Chorus

Verse 2:
Dance floor, seems you're underneath my feet
Everywhere I turn.
I oughta waltz right out of them swingin' doors,
But that's a step I just can't learn.
(To Chorus:)

MUCH TOO YOUNG
(To Feel This Damn Old)

Words and Music by
RANDY TAYLOR and GARTH BROOKS

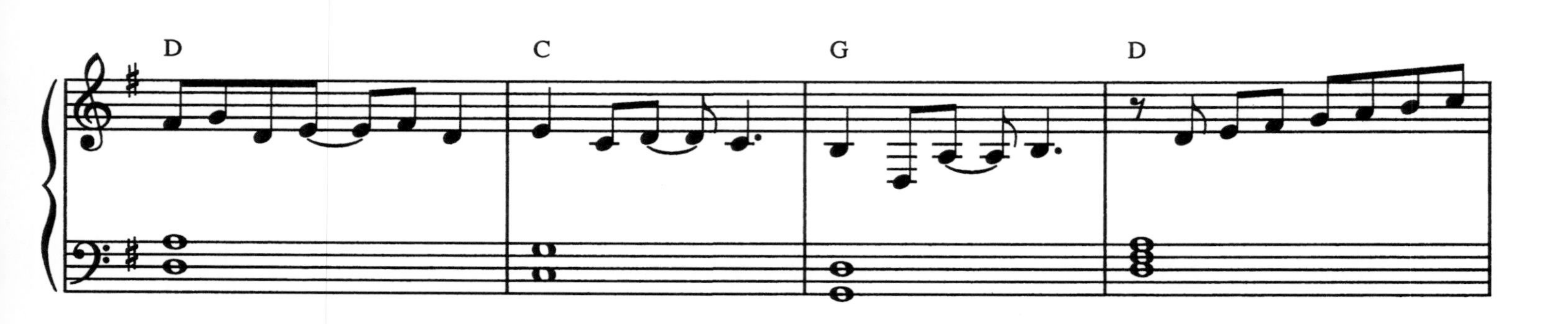

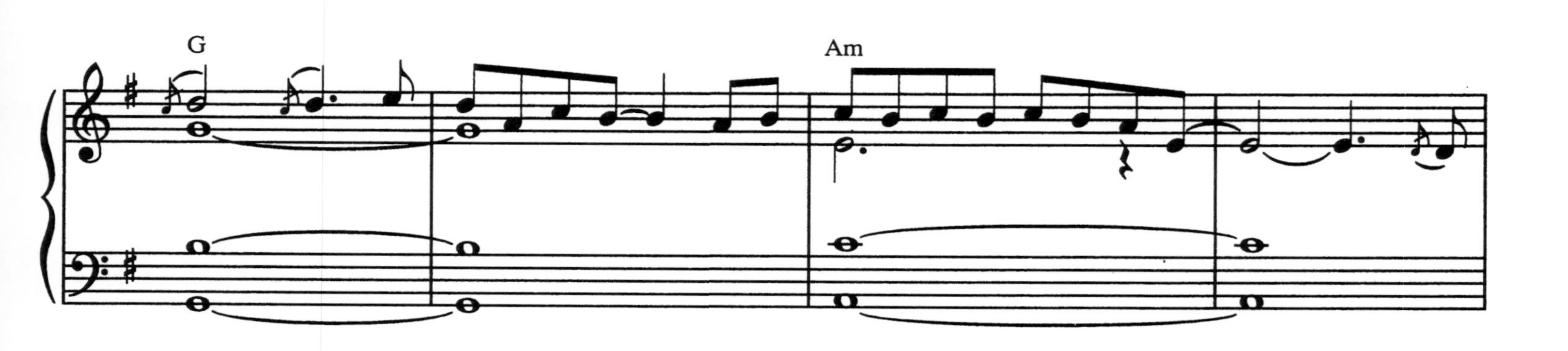

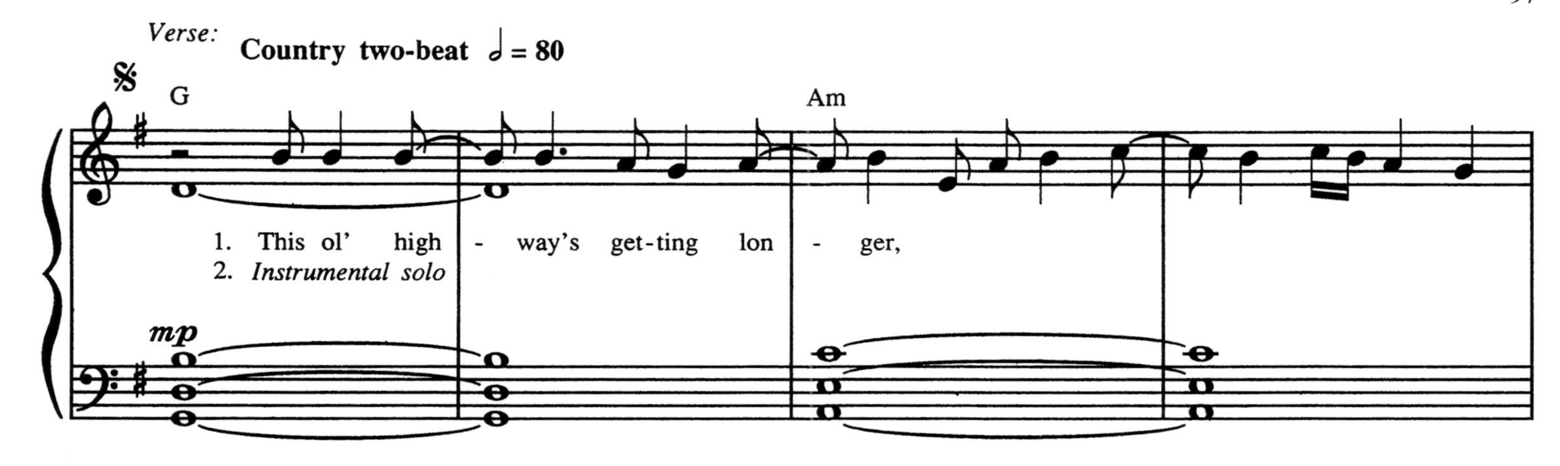
Verse:
Country two-beat 𝅗𝅥 = 80
G
Am
1. This ol' high - way's get-ting lon - ger,
2. Instrumental solo
mp

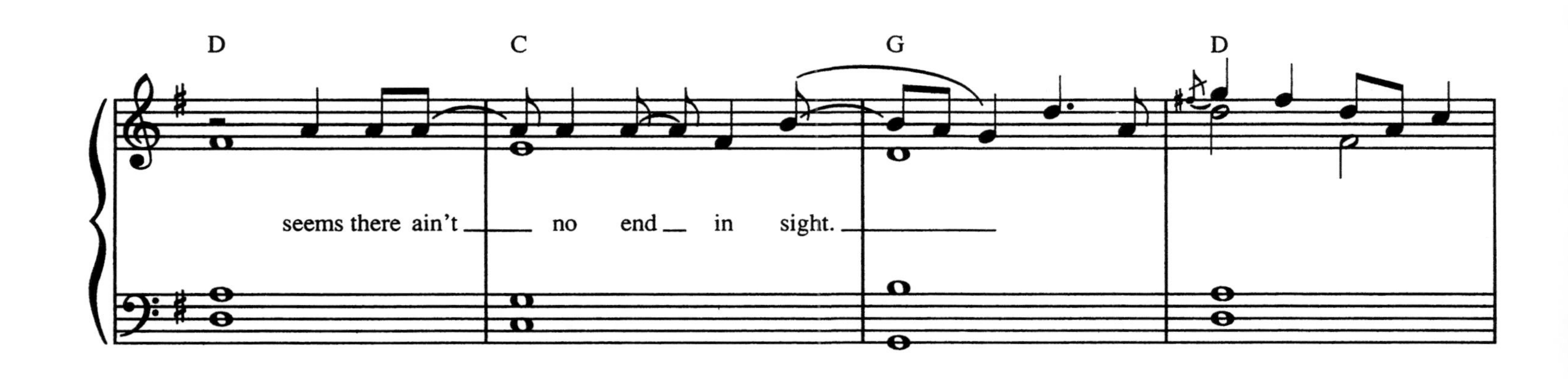
D
C
G
D
seems there ain't no end in sight.

G
Am
To sleep would be best, but I just can't af - ford to rest;

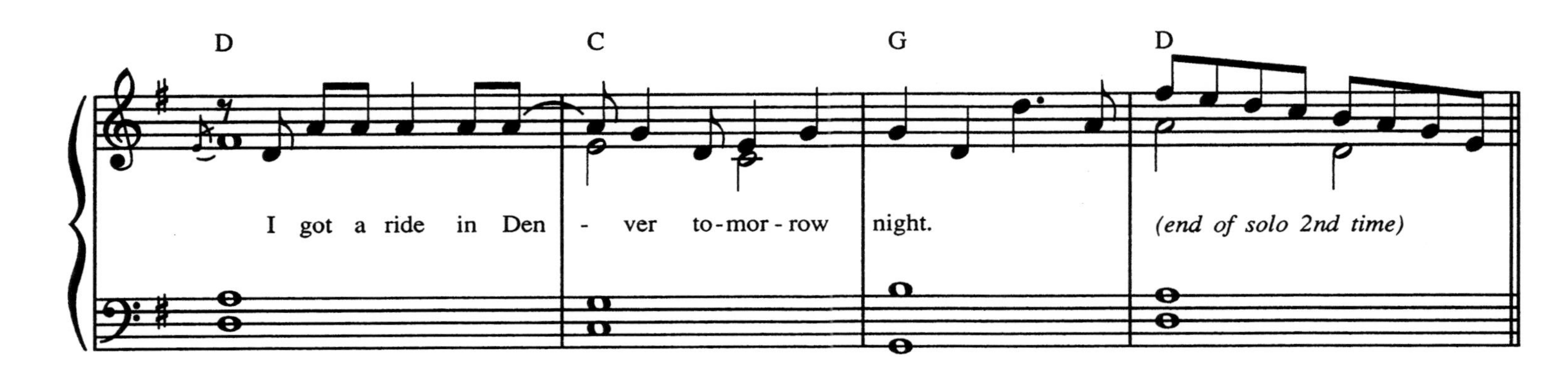
D
C
G
D
I got a ride in Den - ver to-mor-row night.
(end of solo 2nd time)

G
Am
D
mf
I called the house ___ but no _ one an - swered,
for the last two weeks _
C
G
D
G
___ no one's _ been home. ___
I guess she's through with me; _
to tell the
Am
D
C
truth _ I just _ can't see, ___
what's kept the wom - an hold - ing on _ this long. _
G
Chorus:
C
And the white ___ line's get-ting lon - ger, and the
f
G
D/F#
Em
C
D
G
sad-dle's get-ting cold. ___
Now I'm much too young to feel ___ this _ damn old. ___

Verse 2:
(Instrumental solo for 16 measures)
The competition's getting younger;
Tougher broncs, you know I can't recall.
A worn out tape of Chris LeDoux, lonely woman and bad booze,
Seem to be the only friends I've left at all.
(To Chorus:)

LEAVE A LIGHT ON

Words and Music by
RANDY GOODRUM and TOMMY SIMMS

Chorus:
B
B/A
E/G♯
home?
So leave a light on.
Leave a light on for me and I will
mf
A
E
F♯
B
B/A
shine.
And may-be then I could see
you are my
E/G♯
A/G
G
To Coda
A/G
G
A
des-ti-ny.
You and I
keep-ing love a-live till the last tear is cried.
Verse 2:
D
G/D
D
G/D
A/D
D
2. For all time
you're a friend of mine,
and I want to

C/G
G
A
D
G/D
thank you. I thank you for al-ways be-ing there, an-y-where
where on-ly fools would dare. And now, here I am, my friend, reach-ing
F♯
F♯/A♯
D.S. 𝄋 al Coda
𝄌 Coda
out my hand, need-ing you a-gain.
A/G
love a-live till the last tear is cried.
A/D
Ooh,

C/G G C/G G F# F#/A#
ooh, ooh, yeah.
cresc.
Chorus:
B B/A E/G#
cried. So leave a light on. Leave a light on for me and I will
f
A E F# B B/A
shine. And may-be then I could see you are my
Repeat ad lib. and fade
E/G# A/G G A/G G F# F#/A#
des - ti-ny. You and I keep-ing love a - live till the last tear is

THE RIVER

Words and Music by
VICTORIA SHAW and GARTH BROOKS

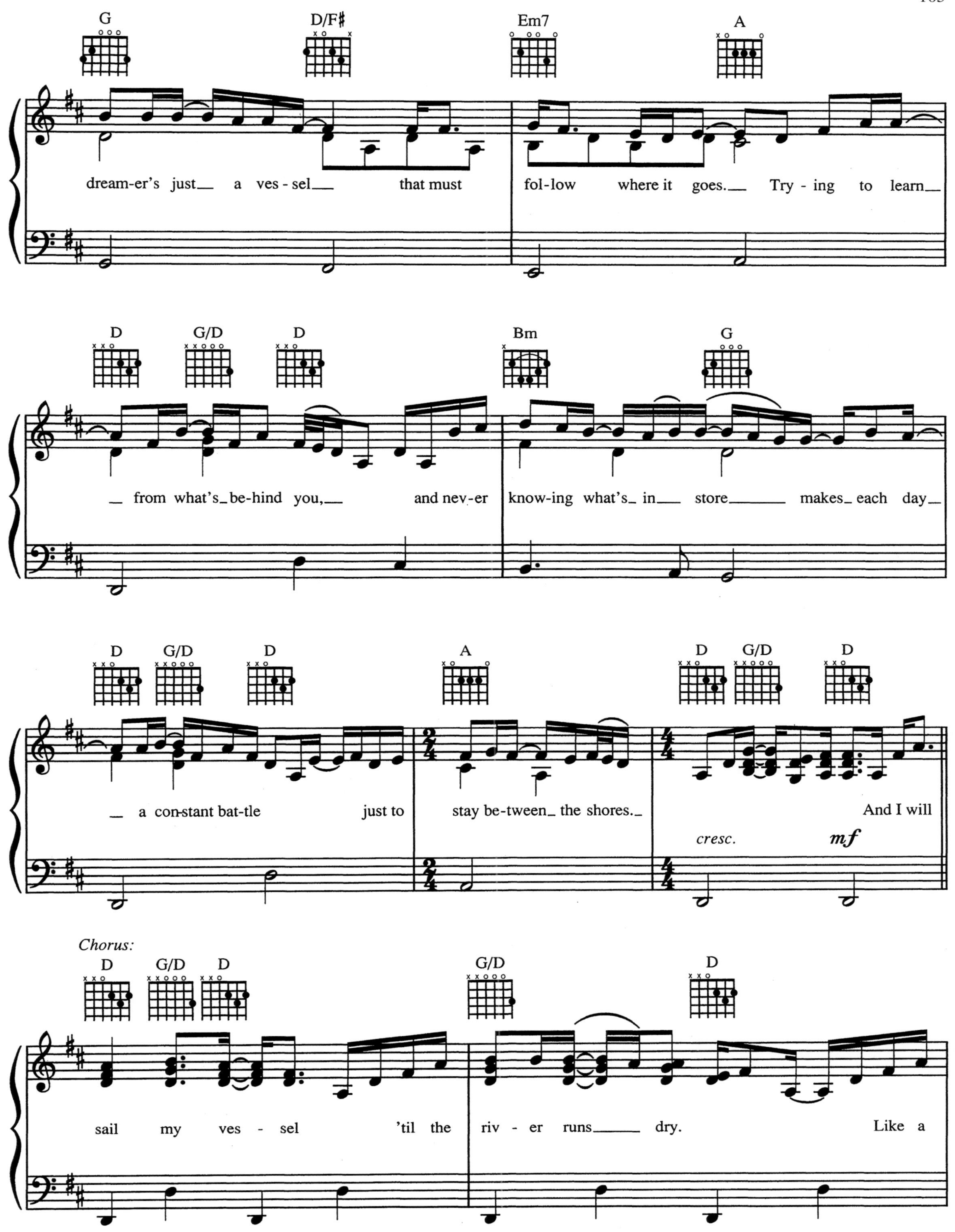
G
D/F♯
Em7
A
dream-er's just a ves-sel that must fol-low where it goes. Try-ing to learn
D
G/D
D
Bm
G
from what's be-hind you, and nev-er know-ing what's in store makes each day
D
G/D
D
A
D
G/D
D
a con-stant bat-tle just to stay be-tween the shores. And I will
cresc.
mf
Chorus:
D
G/D
D
G/D
D
sail my ves-sel 'til the riv-er runs dry. Like a

G
D/F♯
Em7
A
Bm
A/C♯
bird up - on__ the wind, these wa-ter's are__ my sky.____ I'll__ nev - er
D
G/D
D
G
reach my des - ti - na - tion if I nev - er try. So, I will____
D
G/D
D
A
1.
D
sail my ves - sel 'til the riv - er runs_ dry.
dim.
D.S. 𝄋
2.
D
A/C♯
Bm
G
2. Too man-y And there's bound to be__ rough_ wa-ters__ and I

D D/F♯ G Em7 D/F♯
know I'll take some falls. But with the Good Lord as my cap - tain, I can
G Asus
make it through them all. Yes, I will
Chorus:
E A/E E
sail my ves - sel 'til the
A/E E A E/G♯
riv - er runs dry. Like a bird up - on the wind, these
F♯m7 B C♯m B/D♯ E A/E E
wa-ter's are my sky. I'll nev - er reach my des - ti - na - tion

Verse 2:
Too many times we stand aside
And let the waters slip away
'Til what we put off 'til tomorrow
Has now become today.
So, don't you sit upon the shoreline
And say you're satisfied.
Choose to chance the rapids
And dare to dance the tide. Yes, I will . . .
(To Chorus:)

STANDING OUTSIDE THE FIRE

Words and Music by
JENNY YATES and GARTH BROOKS

*L.H. tacet verses 1 & 2 on recording.
**Chords in parentheses are played 2nd time only.

(D)
A D/A A
fools who have to dance with - in the flame, who chance a
F♯m7 D Bm7
sor - row and the shame that al - ways comes with get - ting burned.
E E/D C♯m7 E/B F♯m E/G♯
But you got to be tough when con -
D A F♯m A/G♯ D E7
sumed by de - sire, 'cause it's not e - nough just to stand out - side the fire.
1.
A D/A A D/A
D.S. 𝄋
1. We call them

2.
A

Chorus:
D
Esus
A
D
Esus
Stand - ing out - side the fire.
Stand - ing out - side the fire.

A
F♯m
E/G♯
A
Bm
A/C♯
D
A/C♯
Life is not tried, it is
mere - ly sur - vived if you're

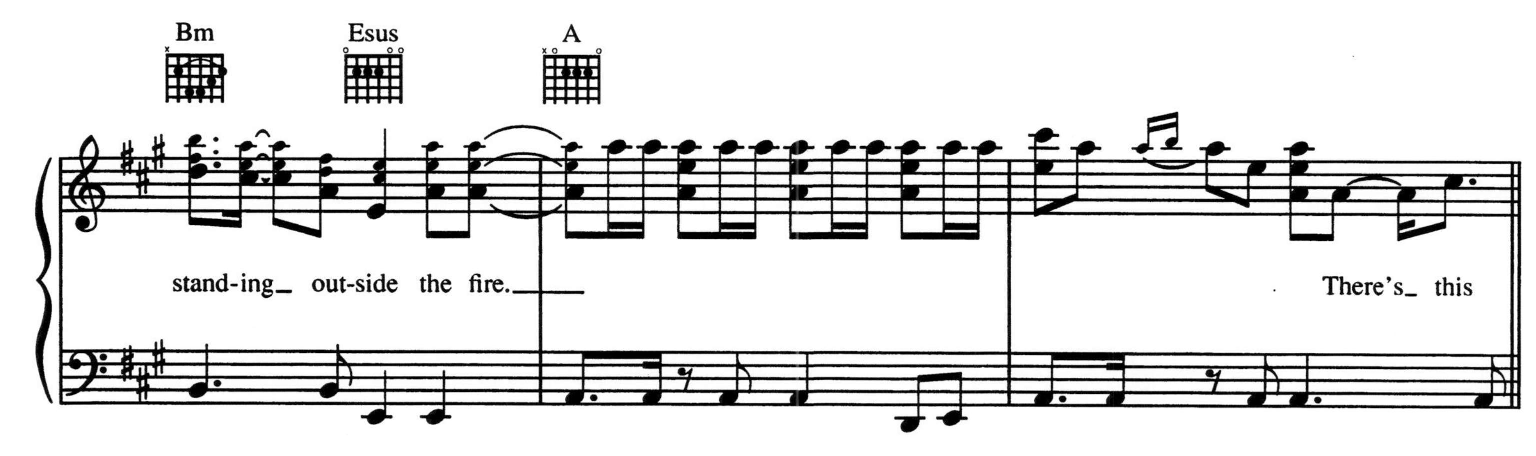
Bm
Esus
A
stand - ing out - side the fire.
There's this

Bridge:
D
A/C#
Bm
love that is burn - ing deep in my soul, con - stant - ly yearn-ing to get
A
D
A/C#
Bm
A/C#
out of con - trol. Want-ing to fly high - er and high-er, I can't a - bide
D
E
N.C.
stand - ing out - side the fire. (Percussion break)
Chorus:
Stand - ing out-side the fire. Stand - ing out-side the fire.
Life is not tried, it is mere - ly sur-vived if you're stand - ing out-side the fire.

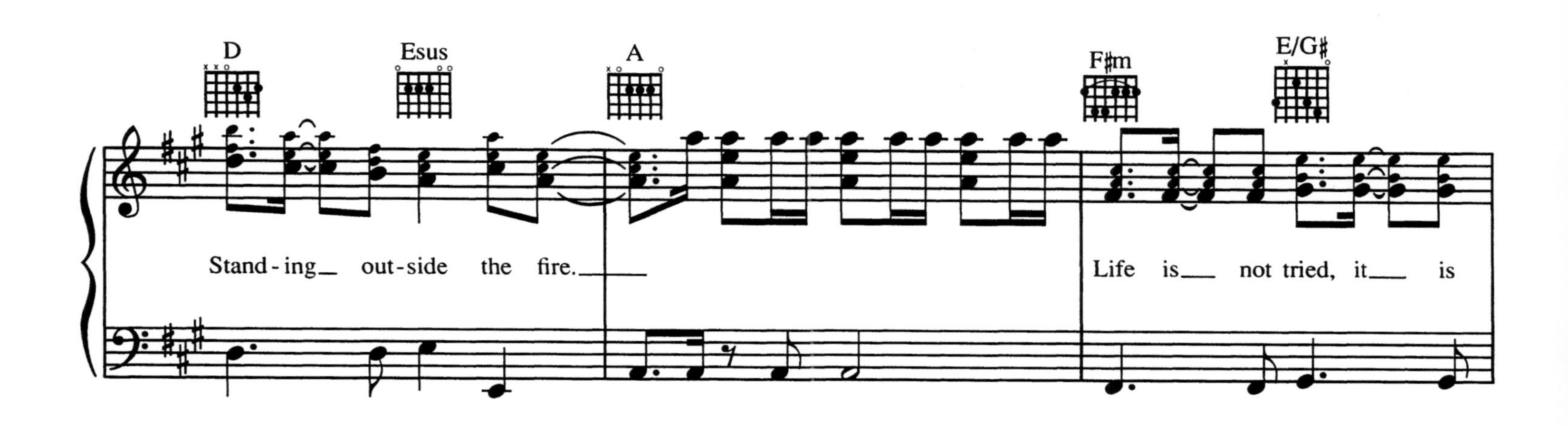

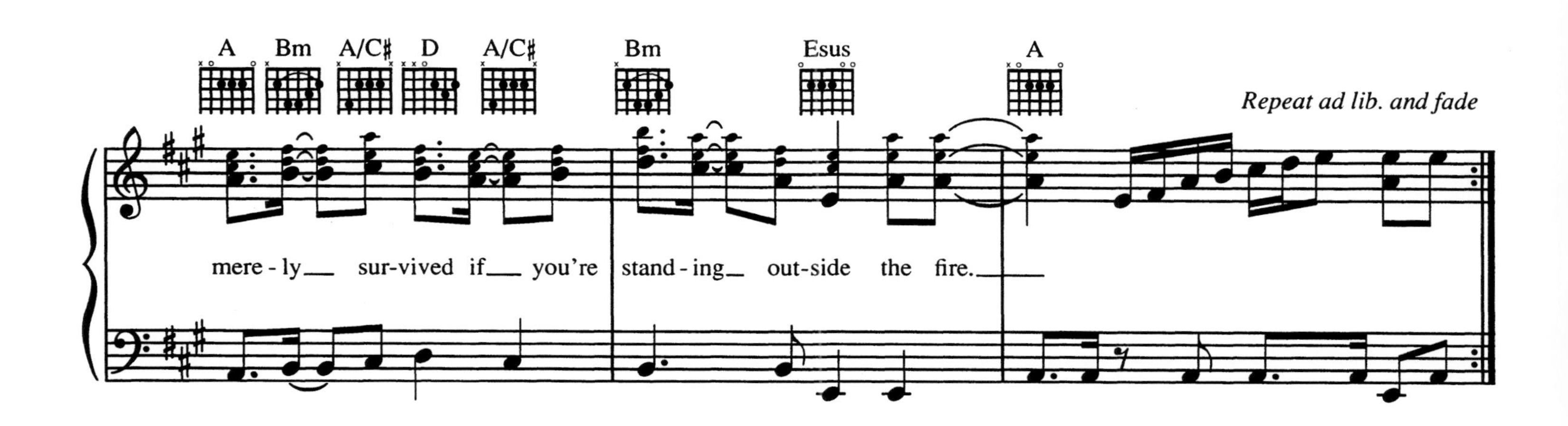

Verse 2:
We call them strong,
Those who can face this world alone,
Who seem to get by on their own,
Those who will never take the fall.
We call them weak,
Who are unable to resist
The slightest chance love might exist,
And for that forsake it all.
They're so hell bent on giving, walking a wire,
Convinced it's not living if you stand outside the fire.
(To Chorus:)

RODEO

Words and Music by
LARRY B. BASTIAN

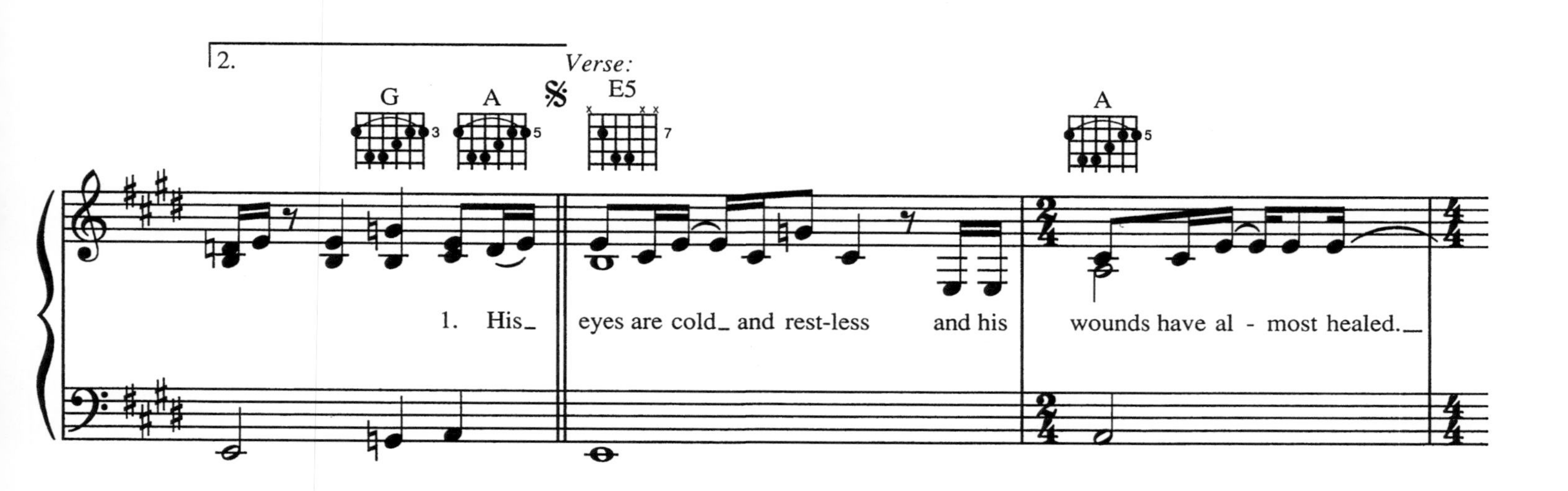

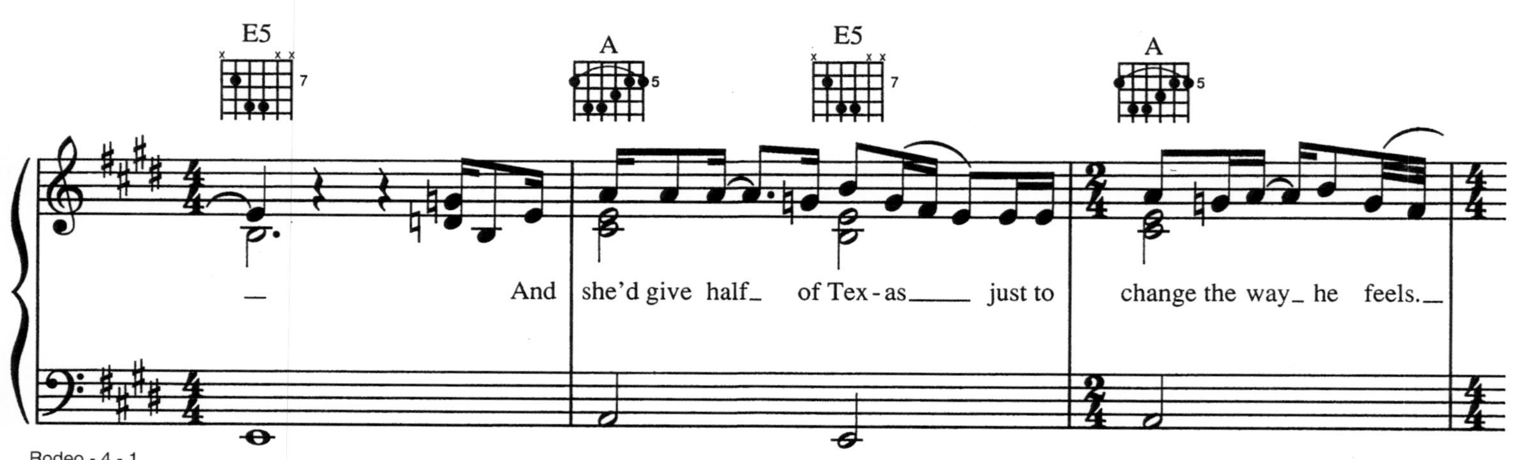

E5
A7
Well, she knows his love's in Tul - sa, and she knows he's gon-na go.
E5
E7
Well, it ain't no wo - man, flesh and blood, it's that
B5
Chorus:
E5
damned old ro - de - o. Well, it's bulls and blood, it's the dust and mud it's the
A5
E5
E7(♯9)
E5
roar of a Sun - day crowd. It's the white in his knuck-les, the gold in the buck-le he'll

B5
D5
B5
E5
win the next go___ 'round._ It's
boots and chaps,_ it's cow-boy hat's,_ it's
A5
E5
spurs and_ lat-i-go.___ It's the ropes___and the reins,_ and the joy_ and the pain,_ and they call_
1.2.
B5
E5
G
A
_ the thing ro - de - o.______
E5
G
A
D.S.
2. She __
3. It'll __

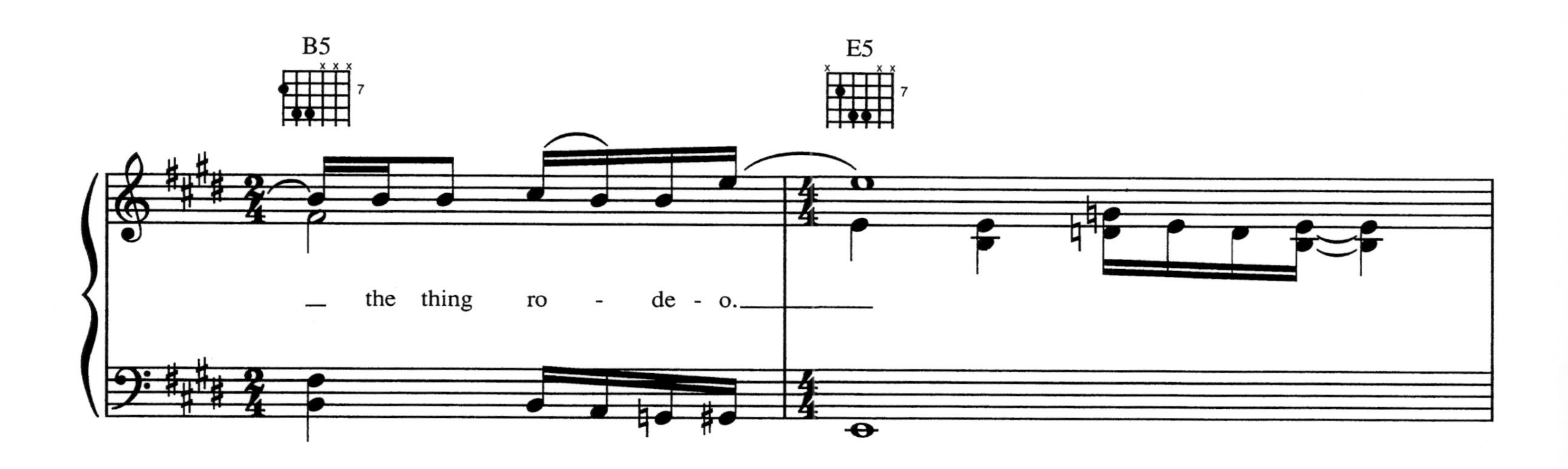

Verse 2:
She does her best to hold him
When his love comes to call.
But his need for it controls him
And her back's against the wall.
And it's "So long, girl, I'll see you.",
When it's time for him to go.
You know the woman wants her cowboy
Like he wants his rodeo.
(To Chorus:)

Verse 3:
It'll drive a cowboy crazy,
It'll drive the man insane.
And he'll sell off everything he owns
Just to pay to play her game.
And a broken home and some broken bones
Is all he'll have to show
For all the years that he spent chasin'
This dream they call rodeo.
(To Chorus:)

SHAMELESS

Words and Music by
BILLY JOEL

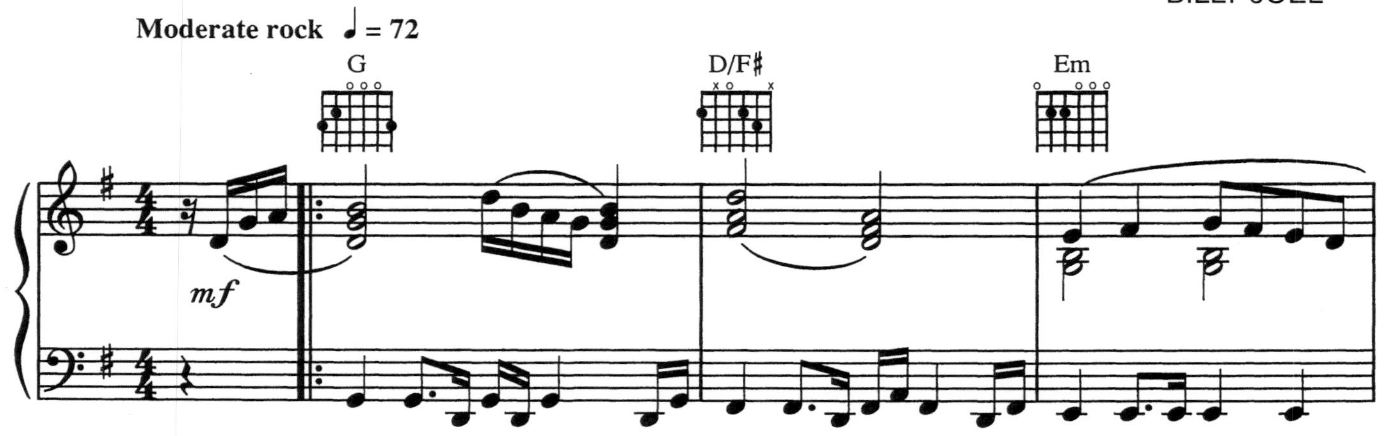

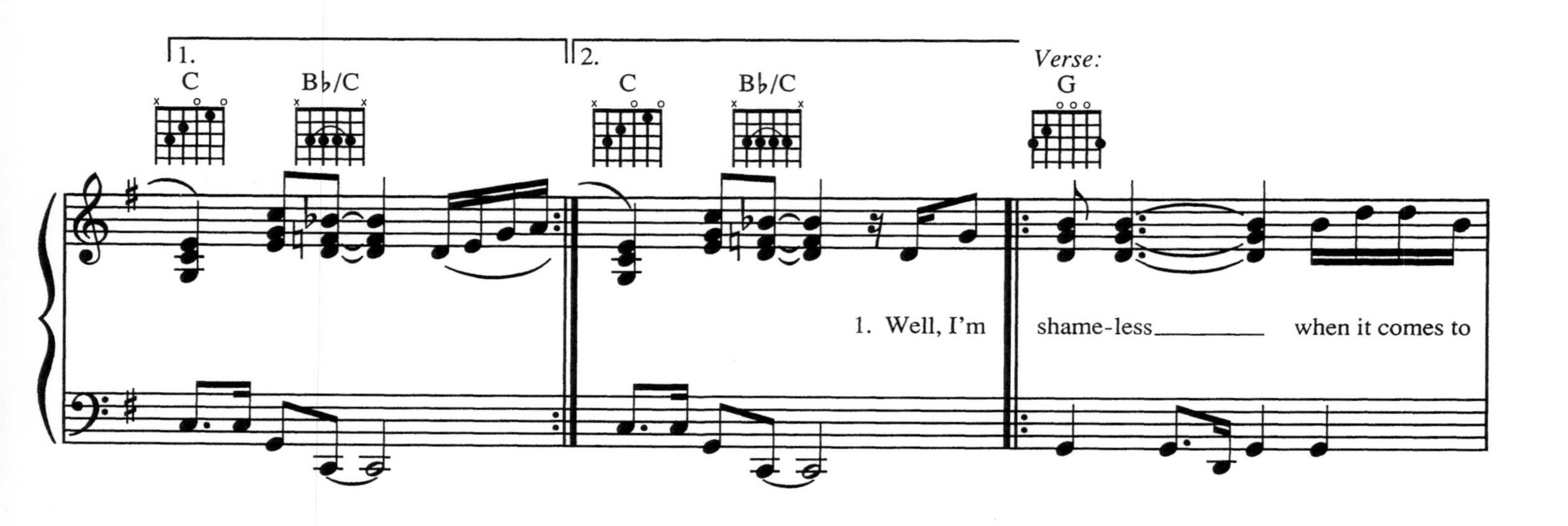

C
B♭/C
G
D/F♯
all.___ And I'm stand-ing______ here for all the world to see,_ oh ba-by, that's what's
Em
C
B♭/C
left_ of me.__________ Don't have ver - y far.________ to fall._____ You know now
D
B7/D♯
Em
Am
G/B
I'm not a man_ who has ev - er been in - se - cure a - bout the world_ I've been liv - in' in.___ I
1.
D
B7/D♯
Em
F
F♯
don't break_ eas - y, I have my pride, but if you need to be sat - is - fied.__ 2. I'm

2.
Em
F
Gm
F/A
Bridge:
B♭
can't walk a - way_ from you.
I have
nev-er let an-y-thing have this much con -
Am7
A♭
E♭
- trol o-ver me._____
I
work too hard to call my life my
own._____
And I
B♭
Am7
made my - self a world___ and it's worked_ so___
per-fect - ly._____
But it's
A♭
Am7
D7
your_ world now, I can't re - fuse.__
I've nev - er had so much to lose._____

G
D/F♯
Em
— Oh, I'm shame-less.___ (Instrumental solo ad lib. . . .
C
B♭/C
G
D/F♯
Em
C
B♭/C
D
B7/D♯
. . .end solo) You know it should be eas - y for a man_ who's strong_ to
Em
Am
G/B
D
B7/D♯
say he's sor - ry or ad - mit when he's wrong. I nev - er lost an - y - thing I've ev - er missed,_ but

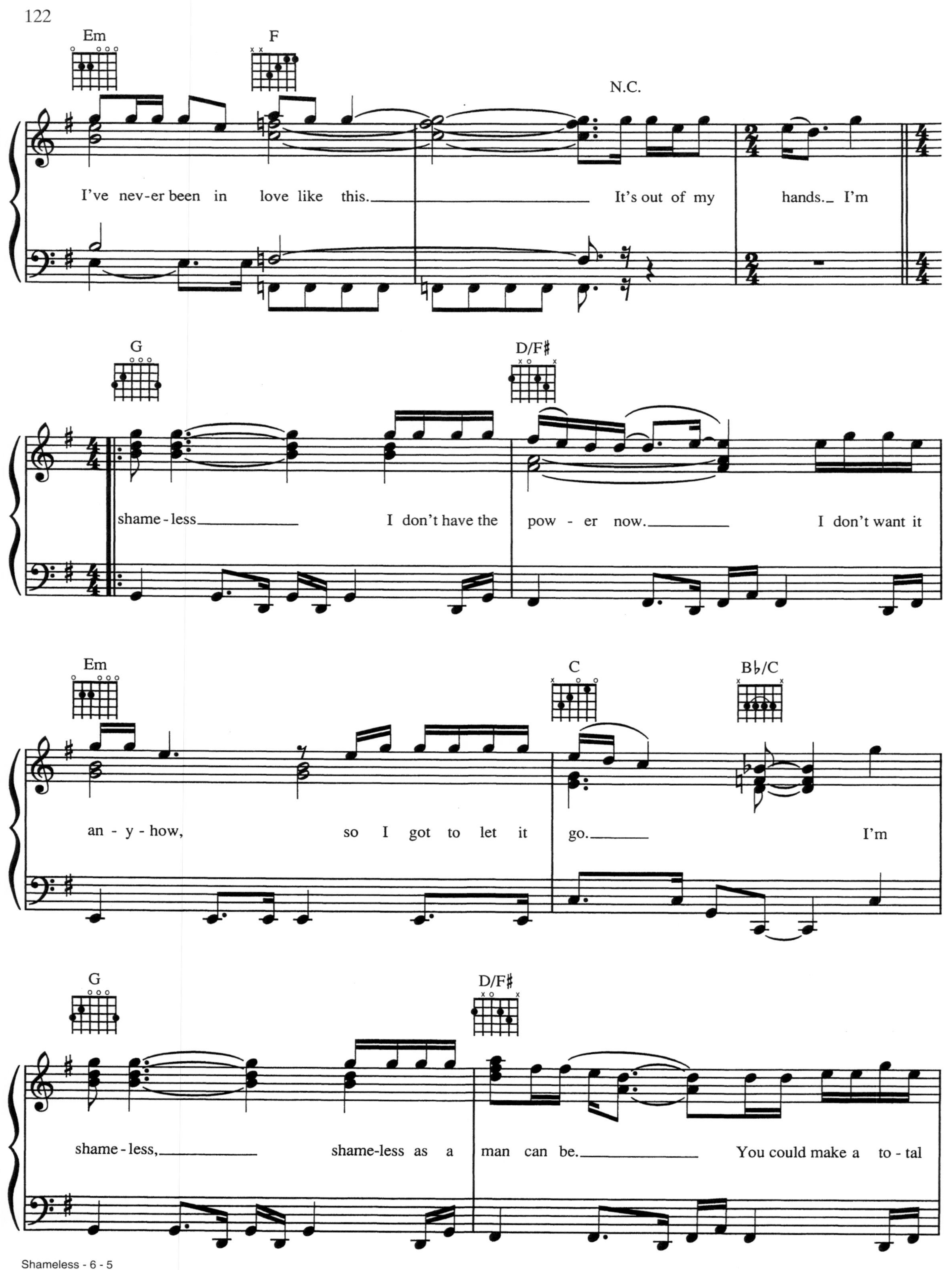
Em
F
N.C.
I've nev-er been in love like this.
It's out of my hands. I'm
G
D/F♯
shame-less
I don't have the pow - er now.
I don't want it
Em
C
B♭/C
an - y - how,
so I got to let it go.
I'm
G
D/F♯
shame-less,
shame-less as a man can be.
You could make a to - tal

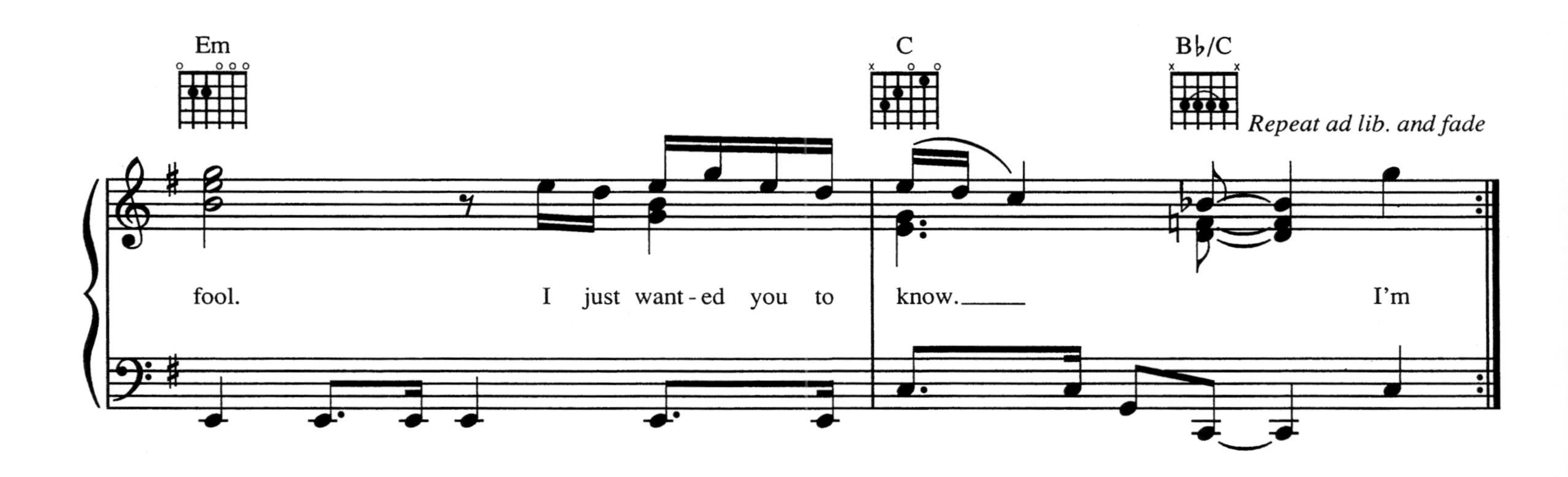

Verse 2:
I'm shameless, oh honey, I don't have a prayer.
Every time I see you standing there,
I go down upon my knees.
And I'm changing, swore I'd never compromise.
Oh, but you convinced me otherwise.
I'll do anything you please.
You see, in all my life I've never found
What I couldn't resist, what I couldn't turn down.
I could walk away from anyone I ever knew,
But I can't walk away from you.
(To Bridge:)

THAT SUMMER

Words and Music by
PAT ALGER, SANDY MAHL
and GARTH BROOKS

E
A
own.
while.
We were a thou - sand miles from
There was a dif - f'rence in her
no-where,
laugh-ter;
F♯m
wheat fields as far as I could
there was a soft-ness in her
see,
eyes;
both need-in' some-thin' from each
and on the air, there was a
D
E
A
oth - er,
hung - er
not know-in' yet what that might
e - ven a boy could rec - og -
be.
nize.
1.
2. 3. 4.
Chorus:
E
2. Till she came to me one
1. 3. She had a need to feel the
thun - der,
cresc.
f

D
A
to chase the light-nin' from the
skies,
to watch the storm, with all its
D
E
won - der
rag - ing in her lov - er's
eyes.
F♯m
E
D
She had to ride the heat of
pas - sion,
like a com - et burn - in'
8va
A
D
bright,
rush-ing head-long in the wind,
out where on - ly dreams had

To Coda
1.
D.S.
E
A
D/A
A
been, burn-in' both ends of the
night.
3. That sum-mer wind_ was all a -
mf
2.
A
D
E
3
3
night.
A
D.S. al Coda
dim.
4. I of-ten think_ a-bout_ that
mf
Coda
A
D
night.
Rush-ing head-long in the wind,___ out where on - ly dreams have

Verse 3:
That summer wind was all around me;
Nothin' between us but the night.
And when I told her that I'd never,
She softly whispered, "That's alright."
And then I watched her hands of leather
Turn to velvet in a touch.
There's never been another summer
When I have ever learned so much.

Chorus 2:
We had a need to feel the thunder,
To chase the lightning from the skies,
To watch the storm, with all its wonder
Raging in each other's eyes.
We had to ride the heat of passion,
Like a comet burnin' bright,
Rushing headlong in the wind,
Out where only dreams had been,
Burnin' both ends of the night.

Verse 4:
I often think about that summer:
The sweat, the moonlight, and the lace.
And I have rarely held another
When I haven't seen her face.
And every time I pass a wheat field,
And watch it dancin' with the wind,
Although I know it isn't real,
I just can't help but feel
Her hungry arms again.

Chorus 3: Repeat Chorus 1, then to Coda.

TWO OF A KIND, WORKIN' ON A FULL HOUSE

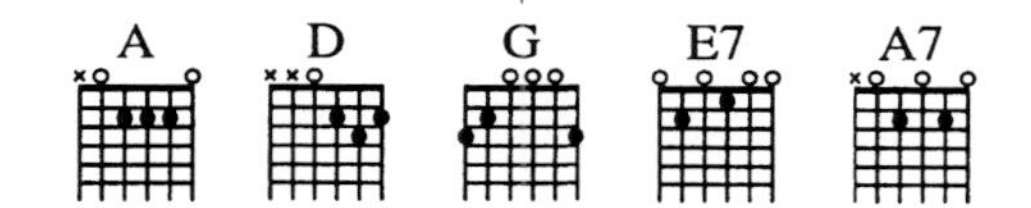

Words and Music by
BOBBY BOYD, WARREN DALE HAYNES
and DENNIS ROBBINS

To Coda
A
Yeah, we're two of a kind, work-in' on a full
1.
D
house.
2. She wakes
2.3.
D
house.
1. Yeah, a pick-
Bridge:
G
-up truck is her lim-ou-sine. And her
D
fa-vor-ite dress is her
fad-ed blue jeans. She
E7
loves me ten-der when the go-in' gets tough. Some-times

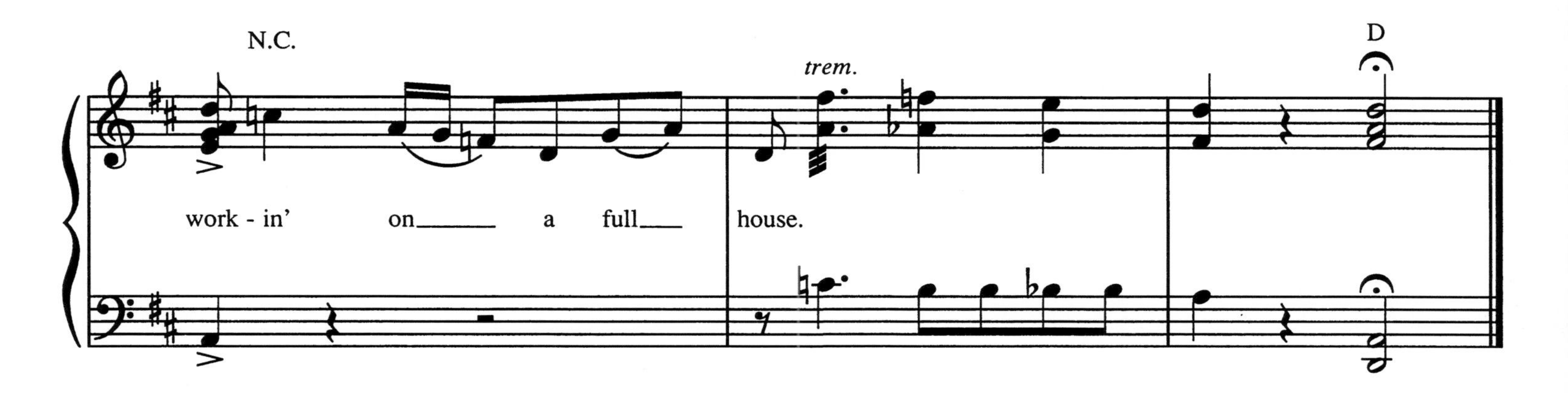

Verse 2:
She wakes me every mornin'
With a smile and a kiss.
Her strong country lovin' is hard to resist.
She's my easy lovin' woman,
I'm her hard-workin' man, no doubt.
Yeah, we're two of a kind
Workin' on a full house. *(To Bridge:)*

Verse 3:
Lord, I need that little woman
Like the crops need rain.
She's my honeycomb, and I'm her sugar cane.
We really fit together
If you know what I'm talkin' about.
Yeah, we're two of a kind
Workin' on a full house. *(To Bridge 2:)*

Bridge 2:
This time I found a keeper, I made up my mind.
Lord, the perfect combination is her heart and mine.
The sky's the limit, no hill is too steep.
We're playin' for fun, but we're playin' for keeps.

Verse 4:
So draw the curtain, honey.
Turn the lights down low.
We'll find some country music on the radio.
I'm yours and you're mine.
Hey, that's what it's all about.
Yeah, we're two of a kind
Workin' on a full house.
Lordy mama, we'll be two of a kind
Workin' on a full house.

THE THUNDER ROLLS

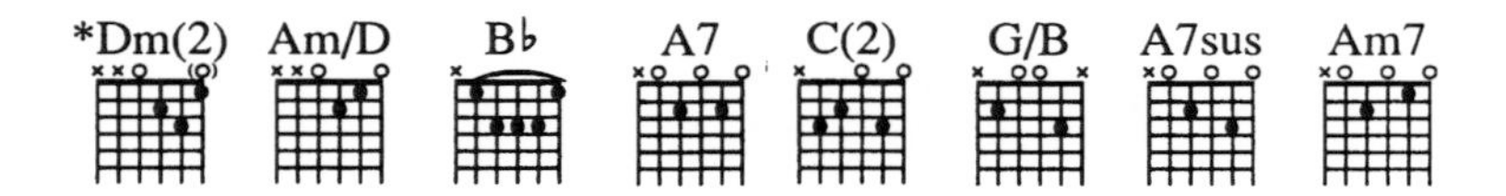

*Alternate between E and F on the 1st string.

Words and Music by
PAT ALGER and GARTH BROOKS

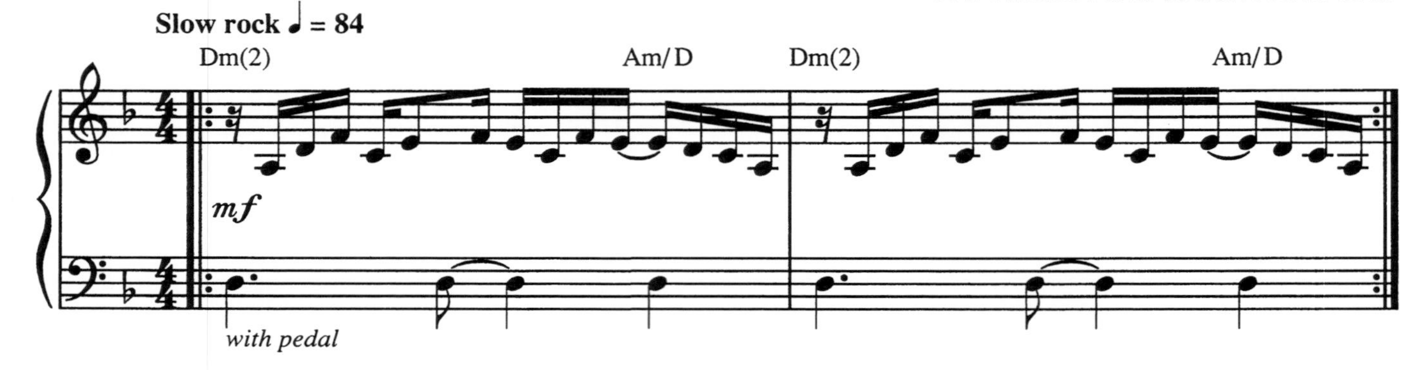

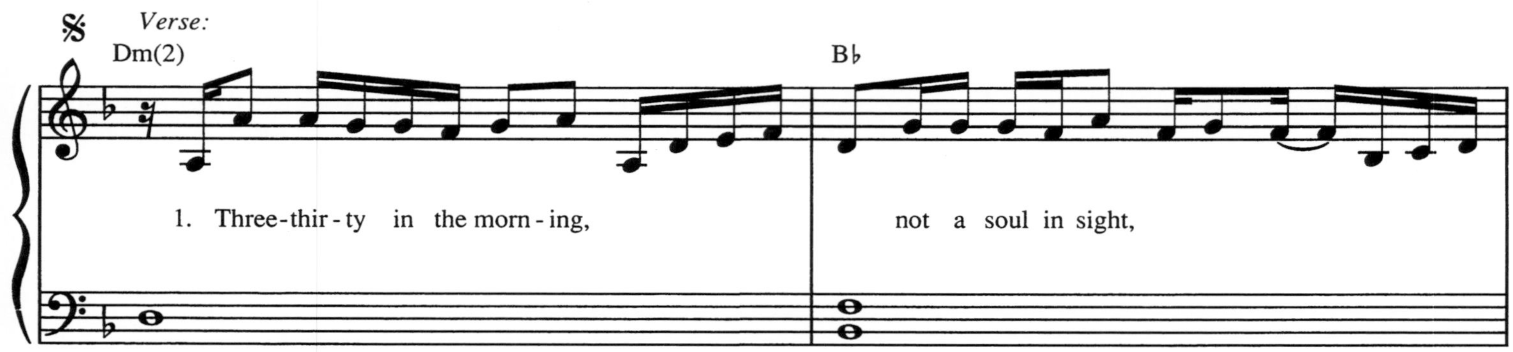

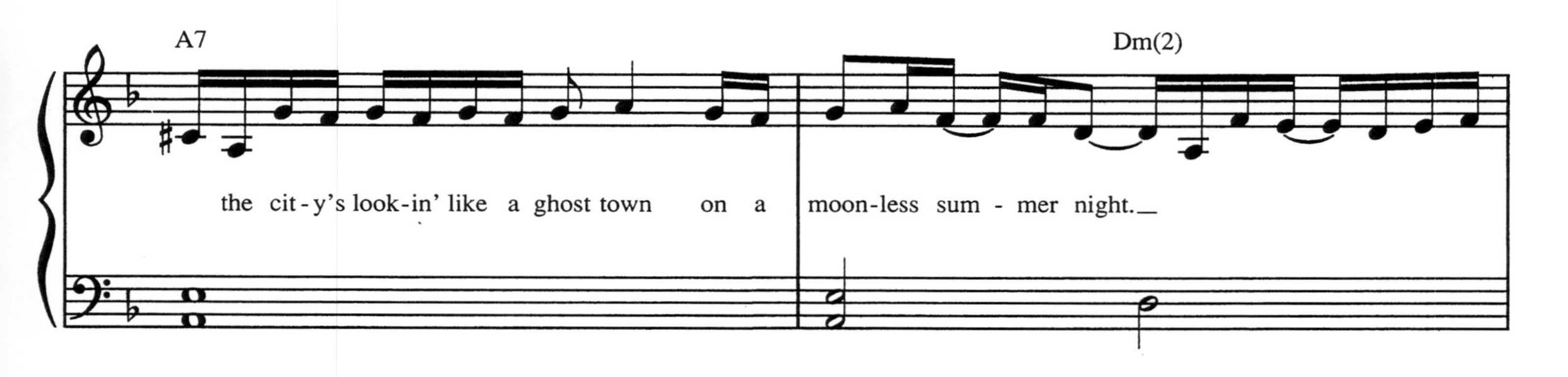

A7
He's head - in' back from some - where that he
nev - er should have been.

Dm(2)
3
C(2)
G/B
And the thun-der rolls,

A7
A7sus
A7
1.
Dm(2)
and the thun-der rolls.
cresc.
mf

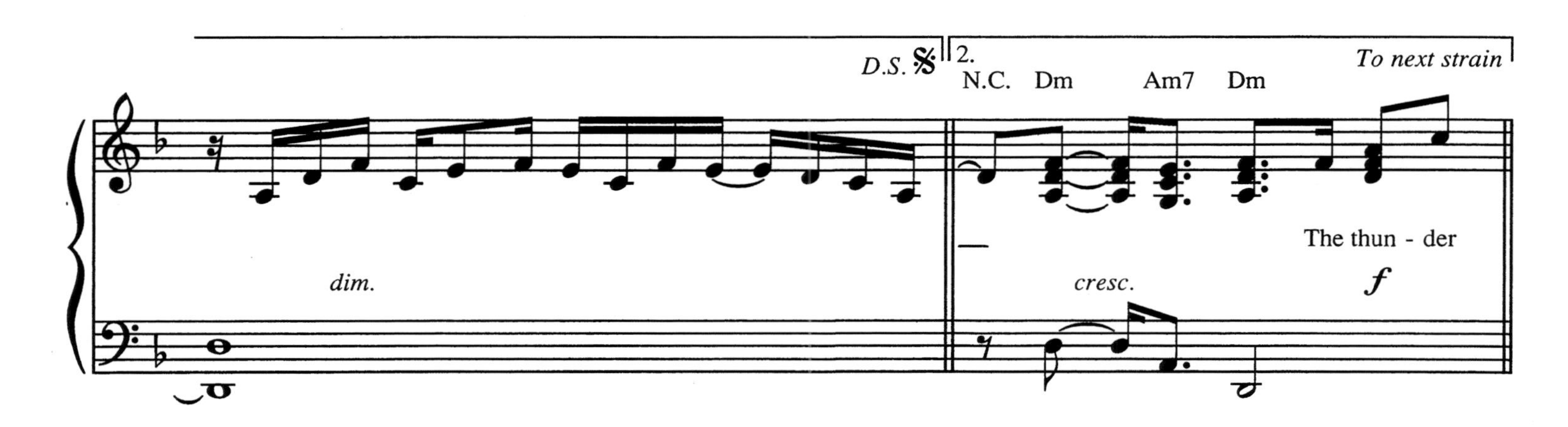
D.S.
2.
N.C.
Dm
Am7
Dm
To next strain
The thun - der
dim.
cresc.
f

3.
Chorus:
N.C. Dm Am7 Dm N.C.
Dm
N.C.
B♭
C
The thun-der
rolls
and the light-nin'

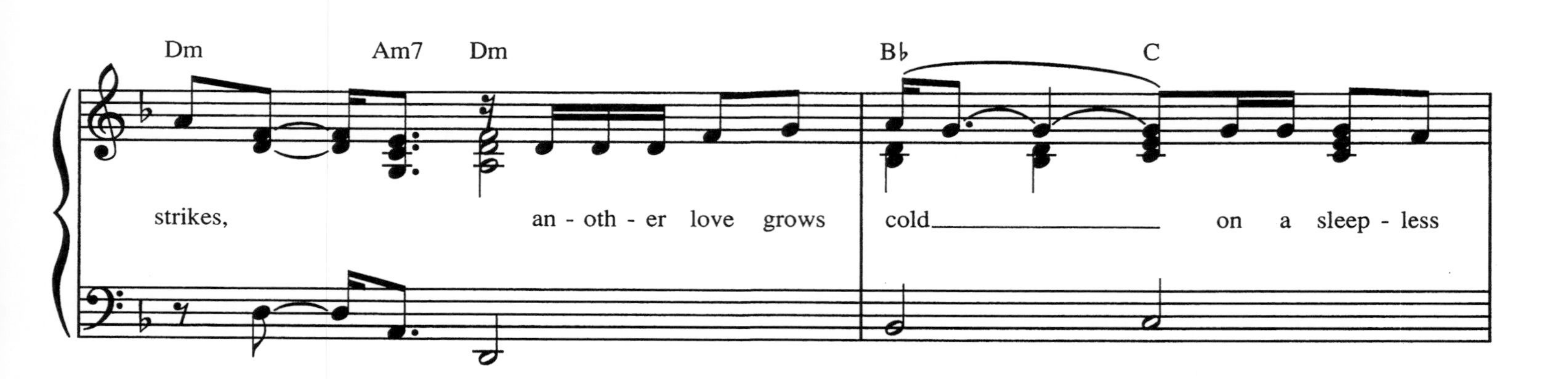
Dm
Am7
Dm
B♭
C
strikes,
an - oth - er love grows
cold
on a sleep - less

A7
A7sus
A7
B♭
C
night.
As the storm blows
on
out of
con - trol,

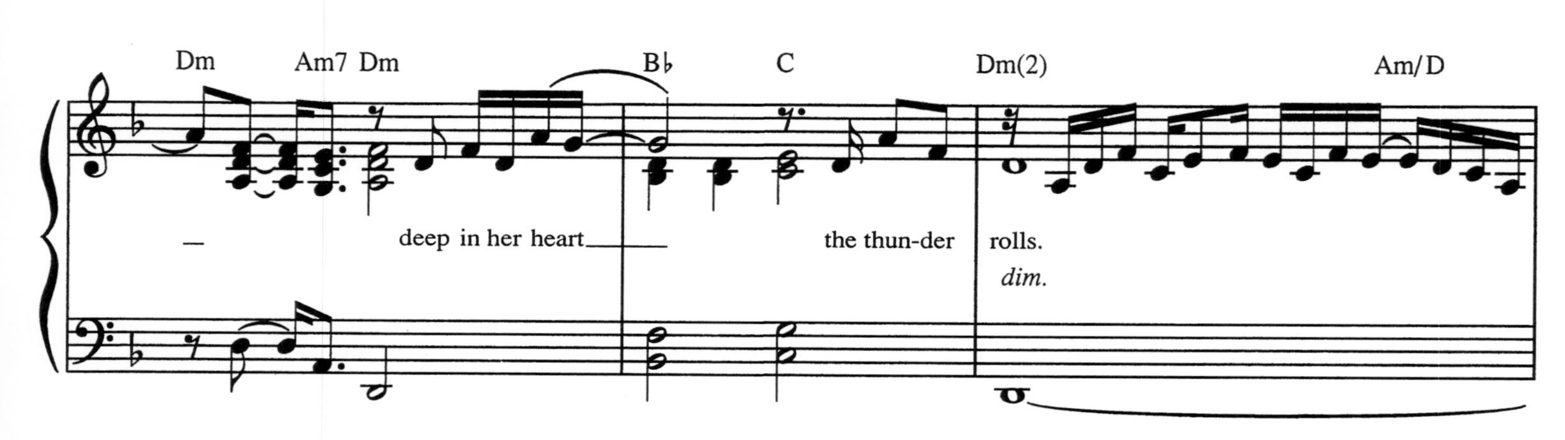
Dm
Am7 Dm
B♭
C
Dm(2)
Am/D
deep in her heart
the thun-der
rolls.
dim.

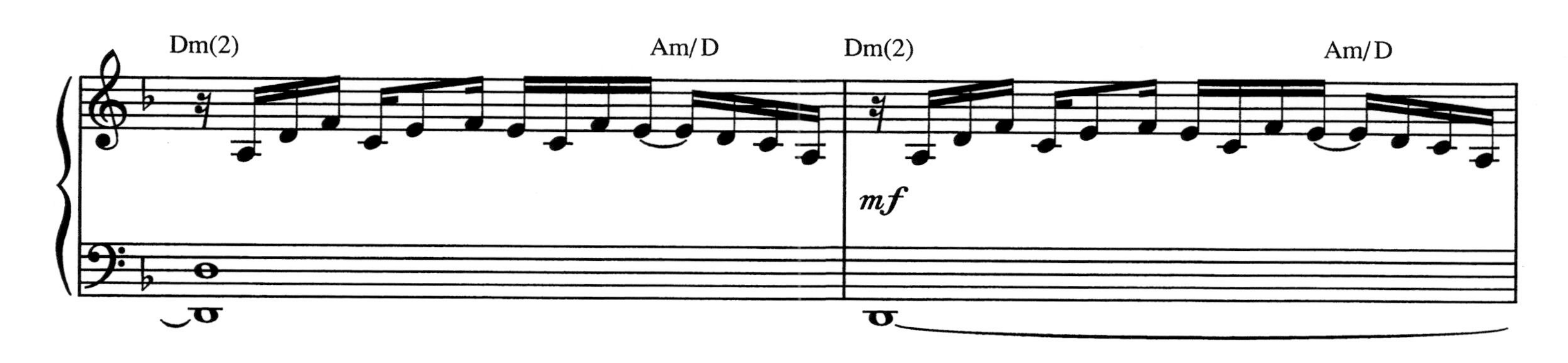

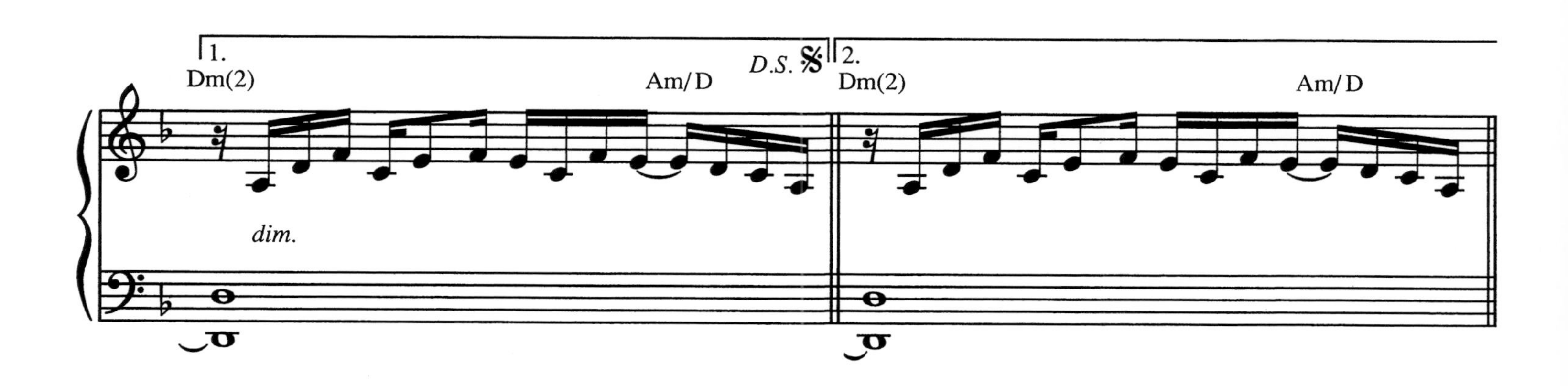

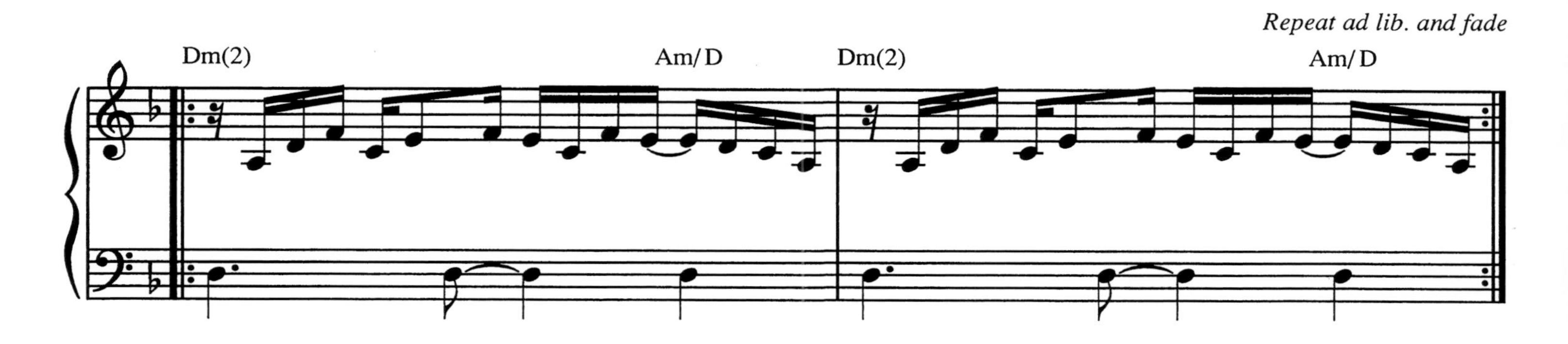

Verse 2:
Every light is burnin'
In a house across town.
She's pacin' by the telephone
In her faded flannel gown,
Askin' for a miracle,
Hopin' she's not right.
Prayin' it's the weather
That's kept him out all night.
And the thunder rolls,
And the thunder rolls.
(To Chorus:)

Verse 3:
She's waitin' by the window
When he pulls into the drive.
She rushes out to hold him,
Thankful he's alive.
But on the wind and rain
A strange new perfume blows,
And the lightnin' flashes in her eyes,
And he knows that she knows.
And the thunder rolls,
And the thunder rolls.
(To Chorus:)

TO MAKE YOU FEEL MY LOVE

Words and Music by
BOB DYLAN

Em7
A
A7
to make you feel my love.
Verses 2 & 3:
D
A/C♯
Am/C
2. When eve-ning shad-ows and the stars ap-pear
and there is no one to
3. I'd go hun-gry, I'd go black and blue,
I'd go crawl-ing down the
G/B
Gm/B♭
D/A
Bm7
dry your tears,
I could hold you for a mil-lion years
av-e-nue.
There ain't noth-ing that I would-n't do
Em7
G/A
D
to make you feel my love.
to make you feel my love.
cresc.

Bridge:
G
D
F♯
G
I know you have-n't made your mind up yet, but I would nev-er do you
The storms are rag-ing on a roll-ing sea, and down the high-way of re-
mf
D
G
D
wrong. I've known it from the mo-ment that we met; there's
gret. The winds of change are blow-ing wild and free, but
Em7
1.
A7sus
A7
no doubt in my mind where you be-long.
you ain't seen noth-ing like me
2.
A7sus
A7
A7sus
A7
yet.
poco rit.

Verse 4:
D
A/C♯
Am/C
4. There ain't noth - ing that I would - n't do;___ go to the ends of the
a tempo
G/B
Gm/B♭
earth for you, make you hap - py, make your
D/A
Bm7
Em7
G/A
N.C.
dreams come true___ to make you feel my love.
rit.
D
A/C♯
Am/C
G/B
mp
a tempo
Gm/B♭
D/A
Bm7
Em7
G/A
D
rit. e dim.
p

TWO PIÑA COLADAS

Words and Music by
SHAWN CAMP, BENITA HILL
and SANDY MASON

E
E7
A
F
F7
B♭
out e - ven know - in'. I packed right up and drove down. Now,
goes on for miles with no in - cli - na - tion to roam.
E
B7
F
C7
I'm on a roll and I swear to my soul, to - night I'm gon - na paint this
I've got - ta say that I think I've got - ta stay 'cause this is feel - in' more and more like
Chorus:
E
N.C.
B
E
F
C
F
town.
home.
So, bring me two pi - ña co - la -
B7
C7
das, I want one for each hand. Let's set sail
with Cap - tain Mor - gan. Oh, and nev - er leave dry land.

E
F
A
B♭
Hey, trou - bles, I for - got 'em, I
bur - ied 'em in the sand. So, bring me two pi - ña co - la -
E/G♯
F/A
F♯m7
Gm7
das. She said good - bye to her good - tim - in' man.
1.
B7
C7
2. Oh now,
2.
bye to her good - tim - in' man.
B
C
Bring, bring, bring me

Chorus:
E
F
two pi - ña co - la - das, I want one for each hand.
B7
C7
Let's set sail with Cap - tain Mor - gan. Oh, and
E
F
A
B♭
nev - er leave dry land. Hey, trou - bles, I for - got
E
F
A
B♭
E/G♯
F/A
F♯m7
Gm7
'em, I bur - ied 'em in the sand. So, bring me two pi - ña co - la -
Repeat ad lib. and fade
E
F
B7
C7
E
F
B
C
das. She said hel - lo to her good - tim - in' man. Bring me

UNANSWERED PRAYERS

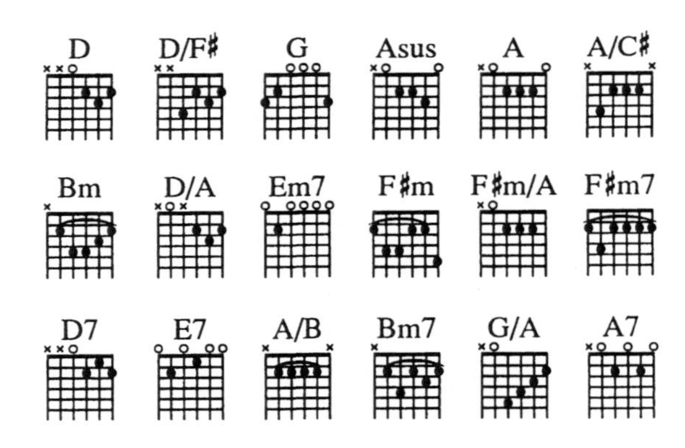

Words and Music by
LARRY B. BASTIAN, PAT ALGER
and GARTH BROOKS

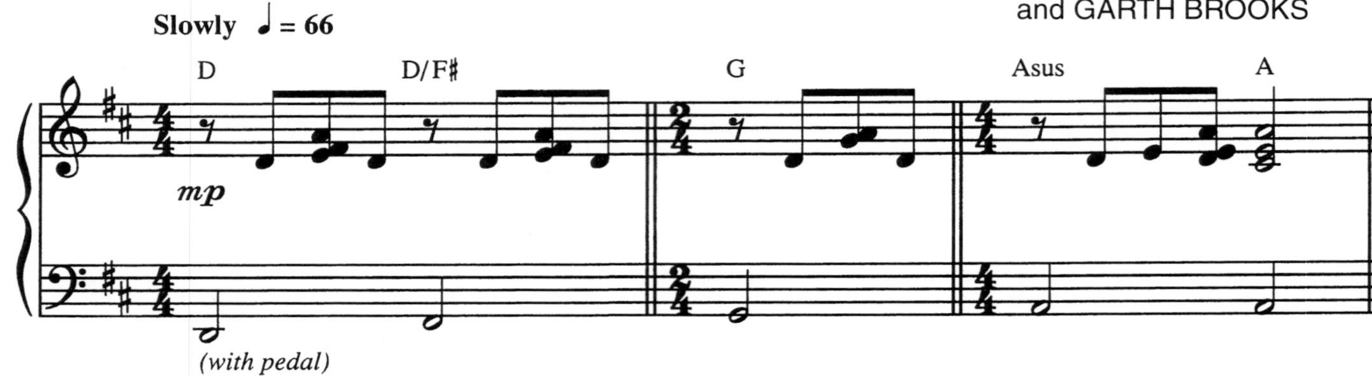

G F♯m Bm F♯m/A G D/F♯
as I in - tro - duced_ them___ the past came back to me.___ and I
if He'd on - ly grant_ me___ this wish I'd wished back then___ I'd

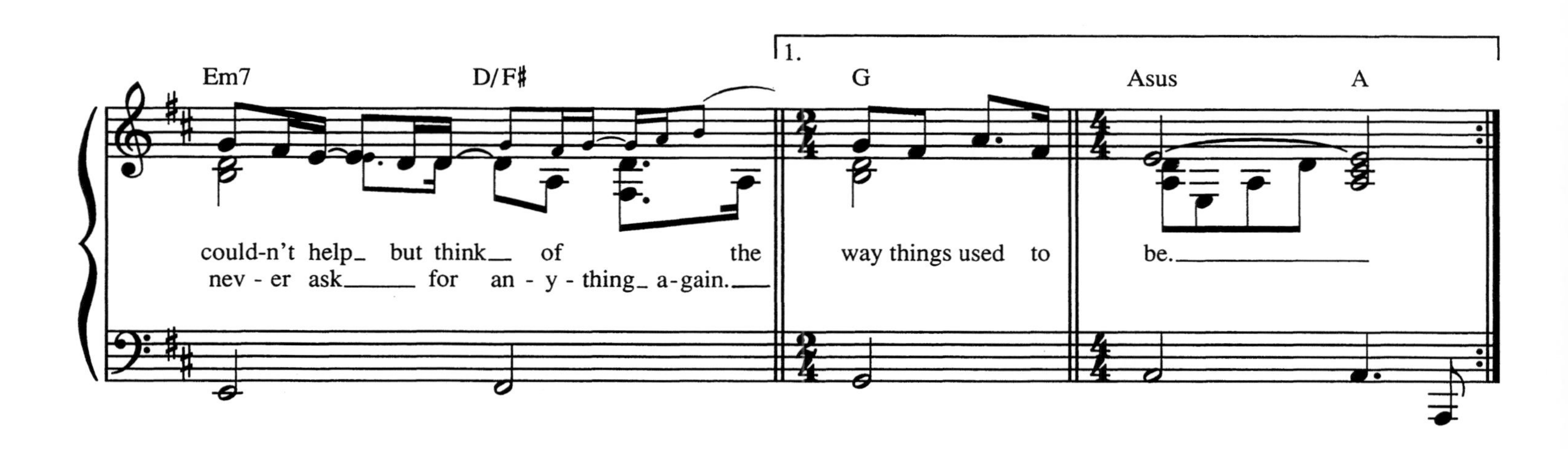
1.
Em7 D/F♯ G Asus A
could-n't help_ but think_ of the way things used to be.___
nev - er ask___ for an - y - thing_ a-gain.___

2.
Chorus:
Asus A D F♯m7
Some-times I___ thank God___ for

G Em7/A A/C♯ D A/C♯ Bm D/A Em7 A
un - an-swered prayers._ Re - mem-ber when you're talk - in' to the Man up - stairs_ that just be-cause_

D
D7
G
E7
He does-n't an - swer does-n't
mean He don't care,
'cause some of

To Coda
D
A/B Bm7
Em7
A
D
D/F♯
G
God's great-est gifts
are un-an - swered prayers.

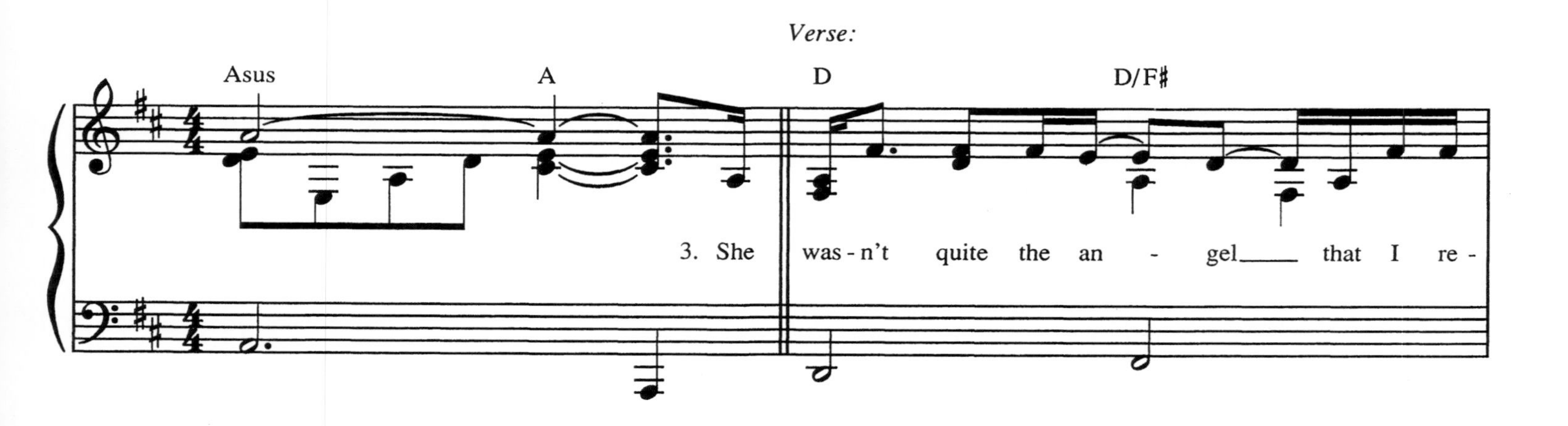
Verse:
Asus
A
D
D/F♯
3. She
was-n't quite the an - gel that I re -

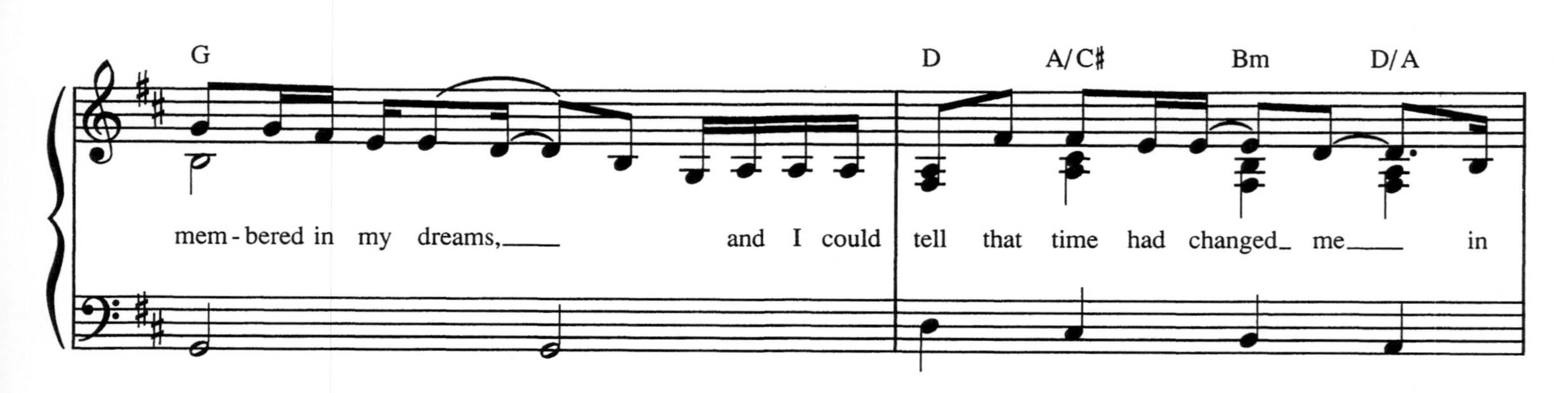
G
D
A/C♯
Bm
D/A
mem-bered in my dreams,
and I could
tell that time had changed me
in

Em7
Asus
A
G
F♯m
her eyes too, it seemed._ We tried to talk a - bout_ the old_ days,_ there was-n't

Bm
F♯m/A
G
D/F♯
Em7
D/F♯
much we could_ re - call._ I guess the Lord knows what he's do - ing af - ter

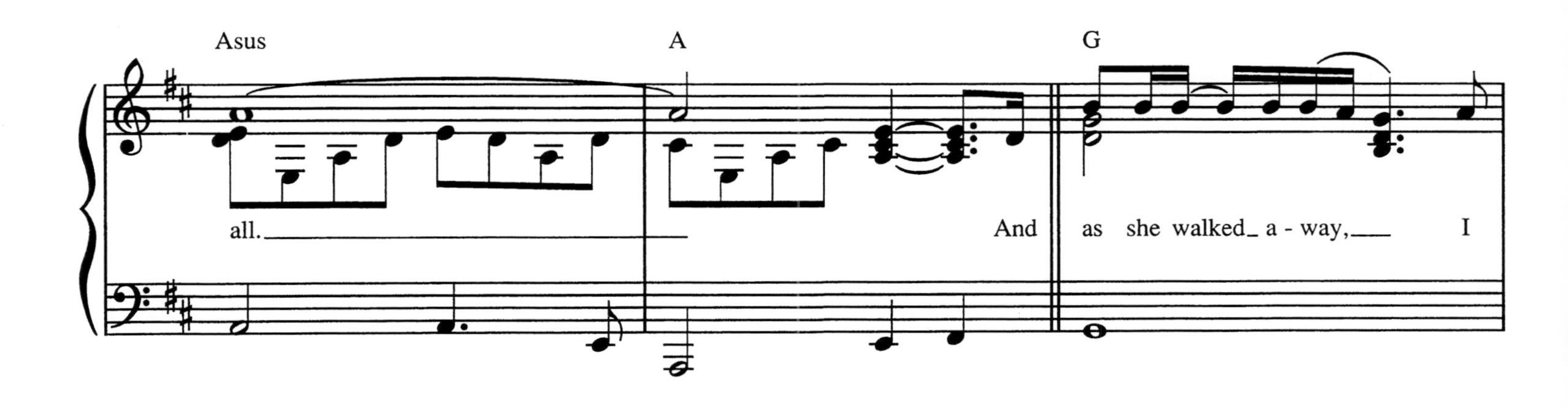
Asus
A
G
all._ And as she walked_ a - way,_ I

F♯m7
Bm7
Em7
D/F♯
looked at my wife,_ and then and there I thanked the good_ Lord for the

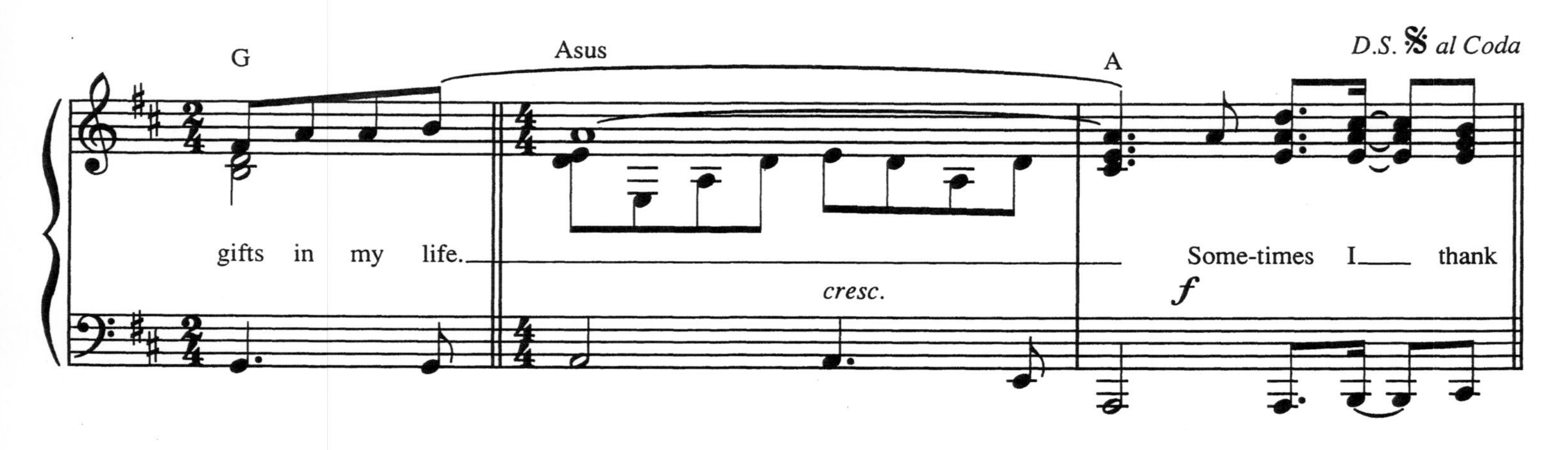
G
Asus
A
D.S. 𝄋 al Coda
gifts in my life.
cresc.
Some-times I thank
f

Coda
Em7
A
D
A/B
Bm7
are un - an - swered, some of God's great - est gifts are all too

Em7
A7sus
A7
D
A/B
Bm7
Em7
A
of - ten un - an-swered, some of God's great-est gifts are un - an - swered prayers.

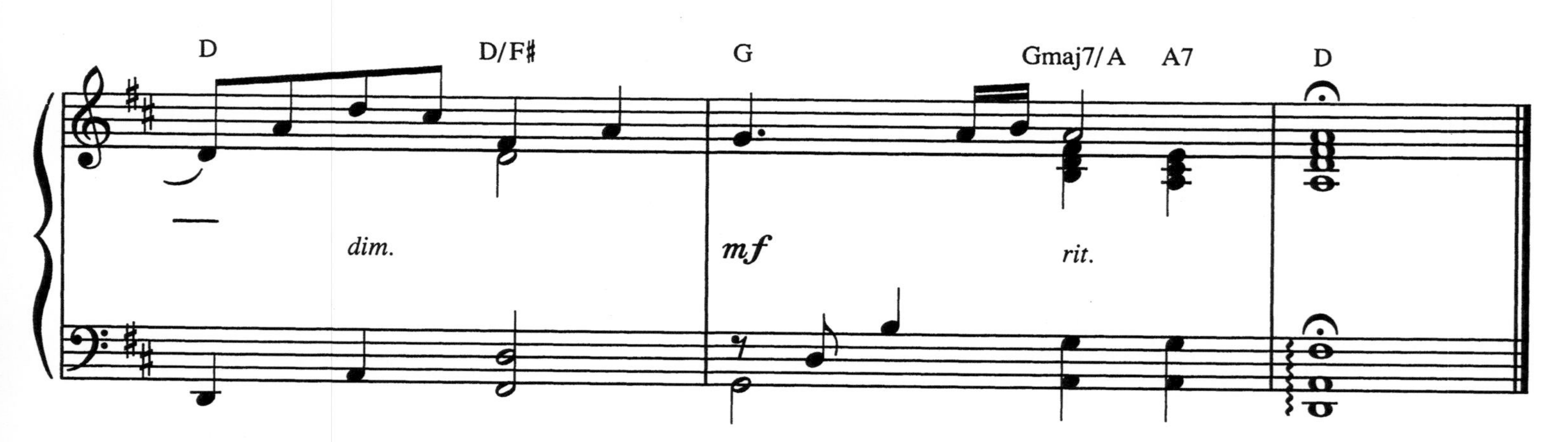
D
D/F♯
G
Gmaj7/A
A7
D
dim.
mf
rit.

WE SHALL BE FREE

Words and Music by
STEPHANIE DAVIS and GARTH BROOKS

Verse 1:
G
C/G
G
C/G
G
1. When the last child cries for a crust of bread, when the
mf
C
D
G
last man dies for just words that he said, when there's shel - ter o - ver the
Em
D
G
C/G
poor - est head, we shall be free. 2. When the
Verses 2 & 3:
G
last thing we no - tice is the col - or of skin, and the

C
D
first thing_ we look_ for is the beau - ty with - in;___ when the
G
Em
D
skies_ and the o - ceans_ are clean a - gain,___ then we shall_ be free._
G
Chorus:
Em
G
A7sus
A7
cresc.
f 1. We shall_ be free,___
C
A7sus
A7
G
A
we shall_ be free.___ Stand straight,_ walk proud,_

1.
D.S. 𝄋
C
D
G
'cause we shall be free.
dim.
mf
3. When we're
2.
To Next Strain
3. 4. etc.
Repeat ad lib. and fade
'cause we shall be free.
'cause we shall be free.
Em
A7
Bridge:
G/B
D/A
Bm/F♯
And when
mon - ey talks for the
ver - y last time, and

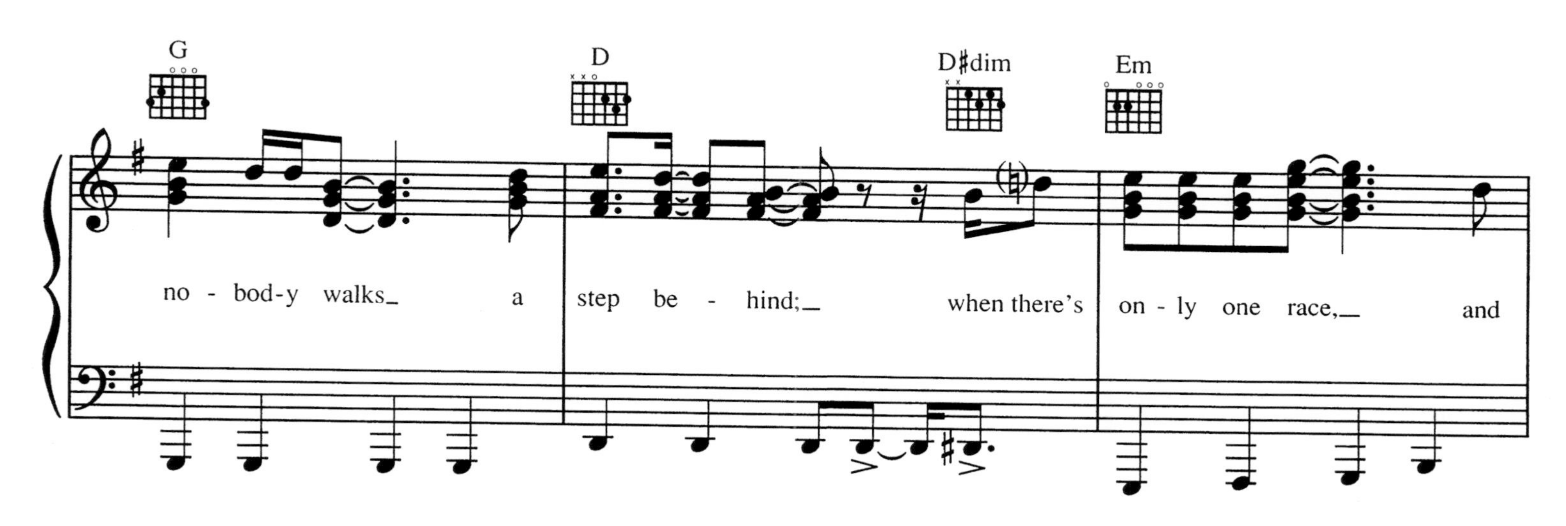

Verse 3:
When we're free to love anyone we choose,
When this world's big enough for all different views,
When we all can worship from our own kind of pew,
Then we shall be free.
(To Chorus:)

Chorus 2:
We shall be free,
We shall be free.
Have a little faith, hold out,
'Cause we shall be free.
(To Bridge:)

Chorus 4:
We shall be free,
We shall be free.
(Stand straight,) stand straight,
(Have a little faith,) walk proud,
'Cause we shall be free.

Chorus 3:
We shall be free,
We shall be free.
Stand straight, (walk proud,)
Have a little faith, (hold out;)
We shall be free.

Chorus 5:
Repeat Chorus 1 and fade

WHAT SHE'S DOING NOW

Words and Music by
PAT ALGER and GARTH BROOKS

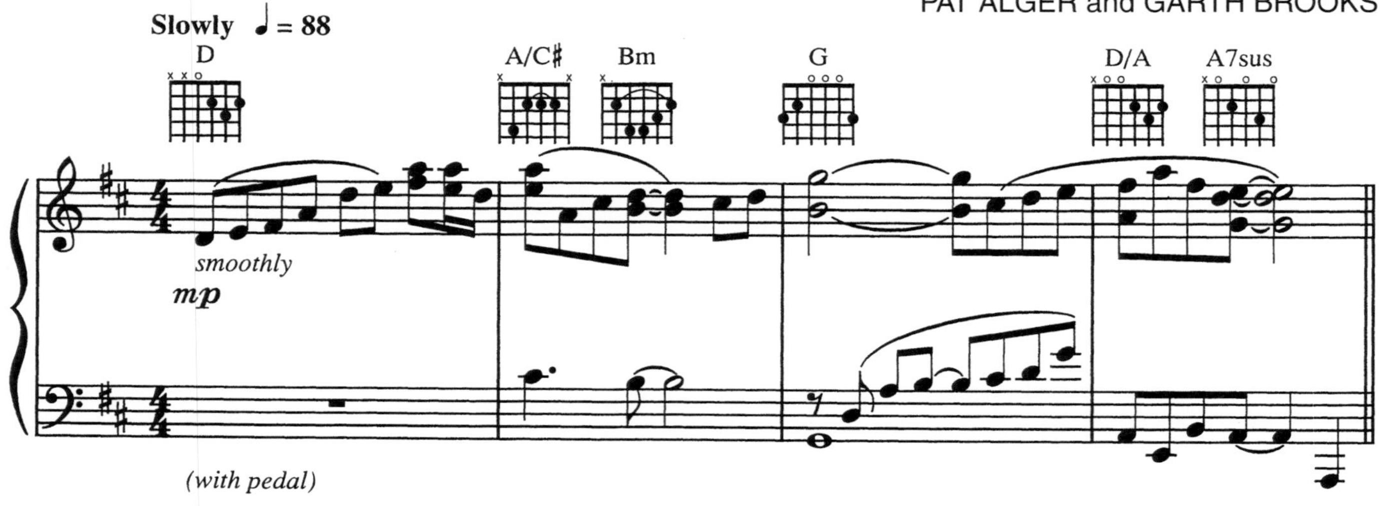

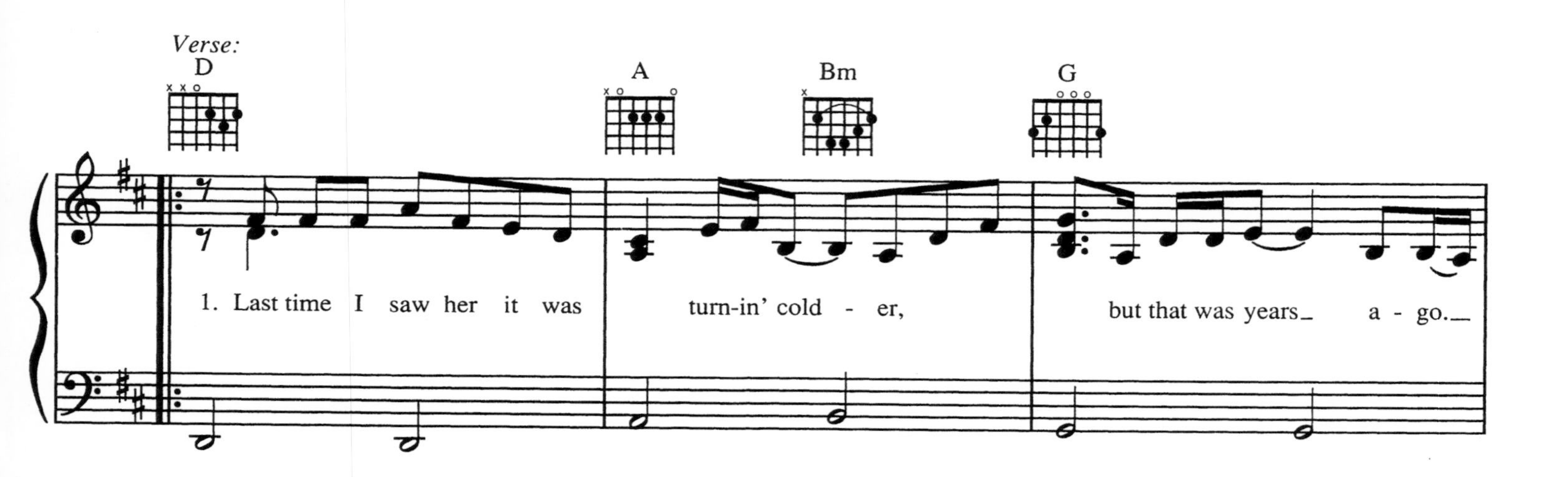

G
D/F#
Em7
A7
G
but where she's now, I don't know.
But there's some-thin' 'bout this time
F#m
Bm
G
D/F#
Em7
F#m/A
A7
of year
that spins my head a - round.
D
A
Bm
G
A7sus
Takes me back,
makes me won - der
what's she do - in' now.
D
A
Chorus:
G
A
Bm
A/B
Bm
A
'Cause what she's do-in' now
is tear - in' me a-part,
fill-in' up my
cresc.
mf

G
A
D
G
G♭m7
mind ___ and emp - ty - ing _ my
heart. I can hear _ her call ___
each time the cold _ wind
To Coda
1.
Bm
D/A
G9
Em7/A
blows. And I won - der if _ she
knows ___
what she's do - in' now.
dim.
D
A/C♯
Bm
G
mp
D/A
A7sus
2.
Em7/A
D.S. al Coda
that what she's do - in' now __

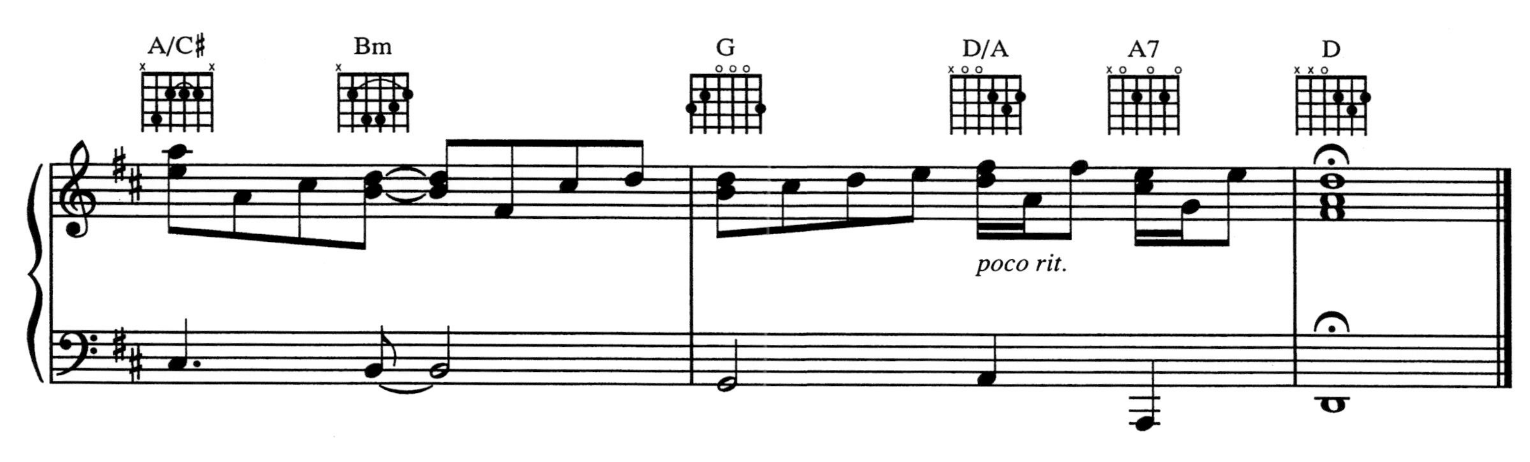

Verse 2:
Just for laughs, I dialed her old number,
But no one knew her name.
Hung up the phone, sat there and wondered
If she'd ever done the same.
I took a walk in the evenin' wind
To clear my head somehow.
But tonight I lie here thinkin'
What's she doin' now.
(To Chorus:)

WHEN YOU COME BACK TO ME AGAIN

Words and Music by
JENNY YATES and GARTH BROOKS

F2
Gsus
G
C2
mer - cy of the sea.
It's been tossed a - bout,
lost and
G/A
Am7
F2
Gsus
G
bro - ken,
wan - d'ring aim - less - ly.
And, God,
B♭6
F(9)/A
1.
Gsus
G
2.
G5
some-how you know that ship
is me.
2.'Cause there's a
in me.
On a prayer,
Chorus:
C
Am7
F
in a song,
I hear your voice
and it keeps me
hang - ing on.

Dm7
G
C
Am7
Oh, rain-ing down, a-gainst the wind, I'm reach-ing out
F
C/E
Dm7
G
To Coda
'til we reach the cir - cle's end, when you come back to me a -
F2
Dm7
G
gain.
3. There's a mo -
Verse 3:
C2
G/A
Am7
ment that we all come to in our own

F2
G7sus
G7
C2
time and our own space,
where all that we've done
we can
G/A
Am7
F2
G5
D.S. 𝄋 al Coda
un - do
if our heart's in the right place.
On a prayer,
Coda
Bridge:
F2
C(9)/E
Dm7
G
gain, and a - gain, I see my yes-ter-day's in front of me,
F2
C(9)/E
Dm7
C(9)/E
un-fold-ing like a mys - ter - y.
You're chang - ing all that is and used to be.

Gsus
N.C.
On a prayer,
Chorus:
D
Bm7
in a song,
I hear your voice
G
Em7
A
and it keeps me hanging on.
Oh, raining down,
D
Bm7
against the wind,
I'm reaching out

Verse 2:
'Cause there's a lighthouse in a harbor shining faithfully,
Pouring its light out across the water for this sinking soul to see
That someone out there still believes in me.
(To Chorus:)

WRAPPED UP IN YOU

Words and Music by
WAYNE KIRKPATRICK

Verse 2:
G
B7
2. How do I need you? Well, can't you tell? I
C(9)
A7
G
need you like a pen-ny needs a wish-ing well. Ba-by, com-
A7
C
Cm
G5
plete-ly, wrapped up in you.
Chorus:
Em
B+
Em7
A7
Ev-'ry now and then when the world that we're liv-ing in is cra-zy, you

Am7
Em7
G
G/B
C
glad - ly hold me and car - ry me through.
Em
B+
Em7
A7
No one in the world's ev - er done what you do for me and I'd be
Am7
Em7
G
G/B
C
Cm
F
sad and lone - ly if there were no you.
Verses 3 & 4:
G
B7
3. How do I love you? Well, count the ways. There
4. How do I love you? Well, don't you know? I

C
A7
G
ain't no num-ber high e-nough to end__ this phrase.__
love you 'bout as deep as an-y love__ can grow.__
Ba - by,__ com-
A7
C
Cm
To Coda
G5
plete - ly__ wrapped_ up in you.__
G
A7
C(9)
Ba ba ba ba ba ba ba__ ba__ ba__ ba ba ba ba ba._
1.
G
F
2.
D.S. al Coda
G
Em
Cm

Coda
G
A7
Ba - by, com - plete - ly
N.C.
wrapped up in you.
G
A7
C(9)
1.3.etc.
2.4.etc.
Repeat ad lib. and fade
G
F
G
Em
Cm
3